SUPERGREENS

SUPERGREENS

LUCY CORNELL

CHARTWELL
BOOKS

This edition published in 2014 by
CHARTWELL BOOKS
an imprint of Book Sales
a division of Quarto Publishing Group
USA Inc.
276 Fifth Avenue, Suite 206
New York, NY 10001
USA

Copyright © 2014
Regency House Publishing Limited
The Manor House
High Street
Buntingford
Hertfordshire
SG9 9AB
United Kingdom

For all editorial enquiries please contact:
www.regencyhousepublishing.com

ISBN-13: 978-0-7858-3206-5

Printed in China

This is a beginner's introduction to a
fascinating look into the health benefits
of 'Supergreens.' It does not, however
encourage self-diagnosis and self-
medication and is not an alternative to
orthodox medical advice and treatment.
The author and the publisher cannot
accept any legal responsibility for any
omissions and errors in this book.

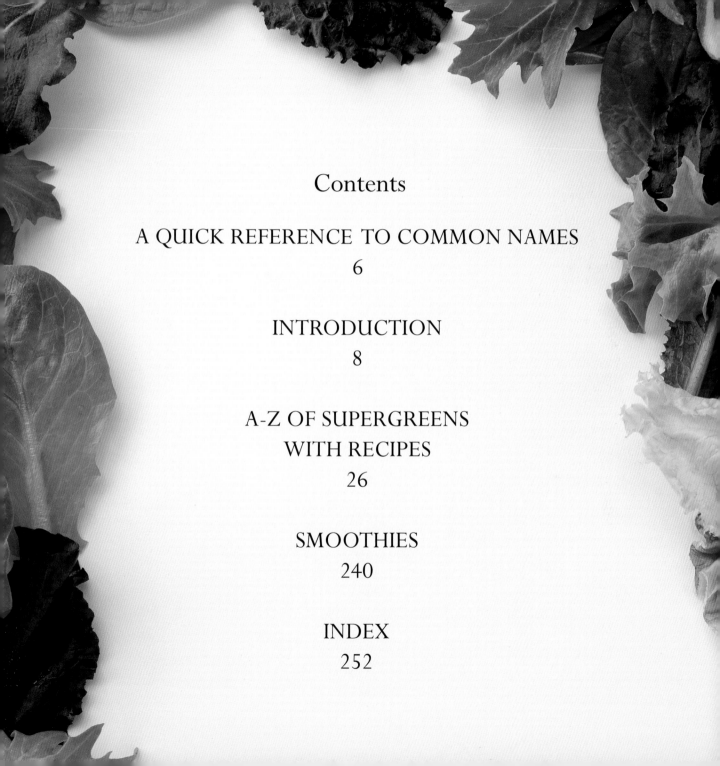

Contents

A QUICK REFERENCE TO COMMON NAMES

INTRODUCTION

Green vegetables bestow amazing health benefits, most of which, as science has progressed, have come to be called 'superfoods,' in that 'magical' properties have become attached to their use.

It seems our ancestors would have agreed with the premise, due to the fact that greens have been eaten since prehistoric times and many of the edible species, known and enjoyed today, have gained importance in cultures and cuisines around the world.

Early man gathered his edible plants by foraging and testing them by trial and error, but as time passed and man evolved, certain plants came to be selected for their nutritional benefits while others were discarded as poisonous or unpalatable. With

ABOVE: The nutritional content of leafy greens brings improvements to hair and skin.

OPPOSITE: Farmers' stands or markets provide a wide range of leafy vegetables.

time, however, and as cooking techniques developed, many of the other vegetables, perceived as bitter or inedible, were rendered palatable and became staples.

It is thought that early man would have eaten large quantities of leafy and other green vegetables per day, these being in plentiful supply, and with few other options. This was fortunate as we now know that these vegetables were loaded with minerals, vitamins and other important nutrients, especially when compared with today's diet,

BELOW: Encouraging children to eat greens can be challenging. Get them involved in food preparation to make them more adventurous in their eating habits.

OPPOSITE: It is a general rule is that the darker the greens the higher the nutritional value.

when modern man may consume only two or three small portions per week.

All vegetables are valuable nutritionally, but it is the green ones in particular which are essential to our health. It is no surprise, therefore, that the old adage, 'eat your greens,' is as relevant today as it has always been. Green vegetables are loaded with minerals, such as iron, calcium, potassium and magnesium, along with vitamins K, C, E and B. They also contain phytonutrients (beneficial chemicals and enzymes) as well as good amounts of fiber.

While today, most of our vegetables are bought in shops and markets, it has become increasingly popular to forage in the countryside for herbs and vegetables as our ancestors once did. It is also surprising that plants, such as sorrel and stinging nettles, have started to reappear in soups and other dishes when they had been all but forgotten until

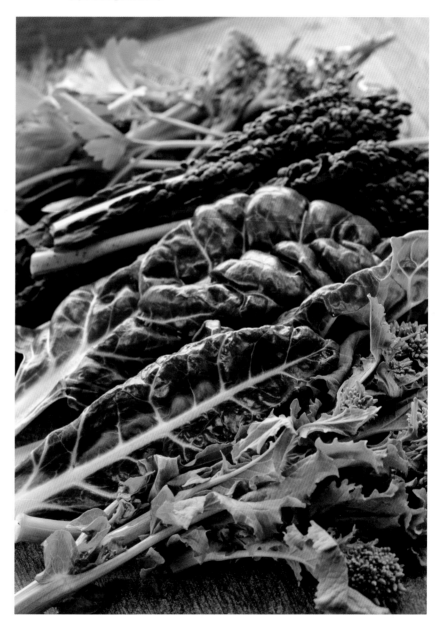

Markets and farm stands are often a great source of fresh, in-season vegetables. Try to choose produce which have been grown locally, which will avoid unnecessary transportation, ensuring carbon emissions are kept to a minimum.

recently. In fact, there has lately been a complete cultural shift in our eating habits, and the once popular fast food outlets, selling foods that are high in sugar and fats, are being replaced by those offering better quality, healthier options, while the growing trend towards the adoption of vegetarian or vegan lifestyles, or simply being more health-conscious, has done much to increase the appeal of vegetables in general.

Most green vegetables, especially when raw, do have a rather bitter taste which, to some, is part of their attraction, but to others it is a taste to be avoided at all costs. But they are a taste well

BELOW & OPPOSITE: While there is no doubt about the considerable health benefits of leafy greens, it is still essential to eat a balanced diet.

worth acquiring and their benefits will become apparent in so many positive ways.

Scientists have discovered that the bitter-tasting compounds present in green vegetables help to ward off diseases such as heart disease and cancer as well as other chronic conditions. These beneficial compounds are, ironically, toxins, but as they are present in relatively small quantities the body is not adversely affected; such toxins are poisonous only if ingested in massive quantities. Generally speaking, it is the youngest vegetables that are the sweetest, and vegetables harvested in the spring also tend to be less strong in taste. While it is best not to cook vegetables for too long, a brief cooking time will

help to reduce the bitterness while preserving most of the nutrients. Some cooks use oils, salt, or acids, such as lemon juice, to enhance the natural flavors of vegetables, at the same time making them more delicious to eat.

Unfortunately, some root vegetables, when sold in supermarkets, have their green tops removed. A good example is the turnip, which is widely sold only as a bulbous root. Fortunately, a little perseverance and research will reveal whole food shops, organic shops, farmers' stands and markets in general where the entire vegetable is available, presenting two culinary options in one.

Greens can be used in a variety of ways, so being inventive in their preparation will make your menus that much more exciting. Greens can be steamed, boiled, sautéed, added to salads, or made into teas, tisanes, smoothies and shakes, while other ingredients can also be added to add color and flavor.

Caution: Most green vegetables are safe to eat, but certain people have intolerances or allergies or are on certain medications that can cause adverse side effects. It is essential, therefore, that you seek medical advice in rare cases such as these.

It must also be stressed that it is the healthiest option to adopt a balanced diet composed of all food types, rather than concentrating on a restricted few which can lead to nutritional imbalance and even, unusually, produce toxic effects.

LEFT: Home-grown vegetables are always guaranteed to be fresh, while involving the younger generation will encourage good eating habits in the future. Always supervise children, however, and make sure hands are thoroughly washed after working in the garden.

RIGHT: A stir-fry of fresh and crunchy greens is a delicious way of getting many of the important nutrients we all require. Other vegetables, fish or meat can be added for extra variety and flavor.

Fruits and vegetables contain lots of vitamins and minerals to keep the body healthy, and the recommendation is to eat five portions a day. What many people do not know, however, is that many fruits and vegetables also contain toxins from being exposed to chemicals, such as pesticides. While it is unlikely that eating raw produce will do you any harm, there is a small possibility that the toxins contained could affect your immune and nervous systems.

Most people are aware of the importance of handling meat correctly, but many believe the risk of food poisoning from vegetables to be low. Washing, using a bowl kept for the purpose, helps remove bacteria, including *E. coli*, from the surface of fruit and vegetables. Most of the bacteria will be in the soil attached to the produce, so removing this

Bok choy has been cultivated in China since the 5th century and today is widely used throughout Asia as well as the rest of the world.

23

soil is of particular importance. Washing is also recommended because of the chemical pesticides used on all regular produce.

Even organic vegetables are susceptible to contamination, more as a result of unsafe practices by people handling them than from organic farming itself.

It is also wise to wash bagged vegetables that have been pre-washed to help eliminate any harmful bacteria that may still be present.

BELOW & OPPOSITE: Greens should be thoroughly washed in cold water under the tap to remove dirt, bacteria and insects and left to drain. Dry salads on clean paper towels or use a salad spinner.

OKRA

BOTANICAL NAME: *Abelmoschus esculentus*
FAMILY: *Malvaceae*

Abelmoschus esculentus, commonly known as okra or ladies' fingers, bhindi or gumbo, is a flowering plant belonging to the mallow family, the edible part of the plant being the green seed pod with its elegant, tapering shape resembling a finger. The plant is widely found throughout the warmer climes of the world, although its precise origin is disputed, with some attributing it to Guatemala, West Africa, India, Bangladesh or Ethiopia.

Okra, regarded as a vegetable but more properly a fruit, with a capsule up to 7 inches long, containing numerous seeds, is a medium-sized plant related to such species as cocoa, hibiscus and cotton. Its flowers have large white or yellow petals, often with red and purple spots.

What is noticeable when cooking okra is the characteristic 'goo' or slime that appears, although brief cooking or stir-frying helps to keep this to a minimum, as, paradoxically, does long, slow cooking and the addition of lemon juice, tomatoes or vinegar.

Okra, although quite subtle in taste, benefits from being cooked with strongly-flavored, spicy ingredients and as a result features heavily in Caribbean, Creole, Cajun and Indian cooking.

In America's deep south, okra is a fine delicacy, and cafés serving their okra specialities are in abundance. It is often served deep fried or wrapped in breadcrumbs.

HEALTH BENEFITS: Due to its mucilaginous properties, okra is reputed to be of benefit to such intestinal problems as irritable bowel syndrome, besides being a general aid to detoxifying the system. Okra's most important medicinal property, however, is its useful mix of soluble and insoluble fibers, which help to stabilize blood sugar levels, benefiting diabetics, and encourage the growth of beneficial bacteria in the gut. It is also said to promote good eye health.

FRIED OKRA

12 okra pods, cut into 1-inch
pieces
1 cup cornmeal
1 beaten egg
Salt and pepper
½ cup vegetable oil

Serves 4

1 Break the egg into a small bowl
containing the okra and leave to
soak for around 10 minutes.

2 Add the oil to a large skillet and
place on a medium to high heat.
Coat the okra evenly in the
seasoned cornmeal to which a
pinch of cayenne has been added.

3 Carefully place the okra, a few at
a time, in the hot oil. Reduce the
temperature to medium and cook
until they are golden brown,
stirring occasionally. Remove and
drain on paper towels. Cook the
remainder and serve.

LEEK

BOTANICAL NAME: *Allium ampeloprasum L.*
FAMILY: *Amaryllidaceae*

The leek is a vegetable related to garlic and onions, and which is, therefore, a little similar in taste, albeit milder. The leeks we use in cooking today are cultivars of *Allium ampeloprasum*.

The edible part of the leek is somewhat erroneously called the stem, which forms itself into a bunch of leaf sheaths, which in turn, similar to an onion, form a tight bulb. Leeks are a favorite vegetable to cultivate, especially by amateurs, in that they are easy to grow from seed and harbor very few pests and diseases.

Virtually all of the leek is used in cooking, but generally speaking the whiter the flesh the milder it is, with the dark-green parts being stronger in taste and tougher to chew.

Leeks can be boiled, steamed, fried or eaten raw in salads. They make excellent soup, with cock-a-leekie being a well-known example.

Today leeks are grown throughout the world, but require fertile, well-drained soil in which to flourish.

HEALTH BENEFITS: Leeks contain many important flavonoid anti-oxidants, vitamins and minerals. It is also thought that allicin reduces cholesterol and can also help to reduce high blood pressure.

COCK-A-LEEKIE SOUP

1 tbsp vegetable oil

1 medium chicken, jointed

6 oz smoked bacon lardons

2½ oz pearl barley

2 carrots, chopped

2 celery sticks, chopped

1–2 leeks, washed and cut into
 thick rounds (reserve green tops)

Splash of white wine

2 bay leaves

Sprigs of thyme

15–20 prunes, pitted

Salt and pepper

Serves 6

1 Heat the oil in a large heavy-based pot until hot. Fry the chicken joints in batches until golden brown, then remove and set them aside. Add the bacon, barley, carrots, celery and leek tops, and sauté for 5 minutes or so until lightly browned. Pour off excess fat.

2 Add the wine and boil rapidly, scraping the bottom of the pan. Return the chicken joints with the herbs and enough cold water to cover. Slowly bring to a boil, then simmer for 40 mins or until the chicken is tender.

3 Remove the chicken to a plate, cover with foil and leave to cool slightly. Discard the thyme sprigs, then leave to stand for a few minutes, skimming off any fat that rises to the surface. Remove the chicken meat from the bones and tear it into large chunks.

4 Simmer the soup with the chicken chunks, the rest of the leeks and the prunes for another 20–30 minutes. Check seasoning. Serve with good bread.

GARLIC SHOOTS

Botanical name: *Allium sativum ophioscorodon*
Family: *Amaryllidaceae*

Allium sativum, commonly known as garlic, is a species in the onion genus, Allium. Garlic is native to Central Asia where it has been a staple for thousands of years. In fact, it is well-known that the ancient Egyptians used garlic for culinary and medicinal purposes.

The garlic bulb (head) divides into single cloves that are usually peeled then crushed or finely chopped before use. But the stem-like shoots or scapes, which are the immature flowering stalks, and which are usually discarded, can also be used in cooking, their flavor being more subtle and milder than the bulb. The stems can be chopped and added to dressings, dips, vinegars and any other recipe you can think of to add an Asian influence or tone down the strong garlic flavors of the dish.

Garlic in general is an essential ingredient in the cuisines of most countries of the world and is often used with tomato, onion and ginger. Oils can be infused with garlic cloves and used to season all types of food.

HEALTH BENEFITS: Garlic is well known to be beneficial to those suffering from a variety of cardiovascular problems. It has antibiotic, antiseptic and antifungal properties and is credited with boosting the immune system, thus helping to prevent common infections. It regulates blood sugar levels and is a remedy for headaches, coughs, rheumatism and asthma.

GARLIC SHOOTS DIP

¾ cup sour cream
¼ cup mayonnaise
Handful fresh garlic shoots, finely
 chopped
½ tbsp fresh parsley, finely
 chopped
Salt and pepper

Serves 4

Place all the ingredients into a medium-sized bowl and mix well. Season with salt and pepper. Serve immediately or refrigerate overnight for a fuller flavor. Delicious with pretzels, chips, toast or crackers.

AMARANTH

BOTANICAL NAME: *Amaranthus tricolor*
FAMILY: *Amaranthaceae*

Amaranth is a very attractive plant, with variegated leaves of green and purple with red or green stems. The colors are particularly vivid, especially when the leaves are freshly gathered.

Amaranth can be found growing across the Americas, Asia and Europe, although it is believed to have originated in South America. The plant was cultivated by the Mexicans for thousands of years, and there is evidence that the Aztecs and Mayans used the plant for religious rituals and for medicinal purposes.

Amaranth has several common names according to location, which include careless weed, Chinese spinach, pigweed and red spinach to name but a few. Both the grain, which is actually the seed of the plant, and the leaves are consumed across the world, although both can be difficult to find in ordinary stores and supermarkets. Fortunately, they are widely available in Asian and Caribbean stores.

HEALTH BENEFITS: Loaded with vitamins A, B6 and C and minerals such as magnesium, iron, manganese, niacin, phosphorus, riboflavin, potassium and zinc, aramanth is high in oxalate.

CALLALOO

1 lb aramanth (callaloo) leaves or spinach

1 onion, chopped

5 cups chicken stock

½ lb diced salt beef with the fat removed

6 tbsp shallots, finely minced

¼ tsp chopped thyme leaves

1 green chili, finely chopped.

½ lb crabmeat

1 cup okra

Salt and black pepper

Serves 6

1 Roughly chop the aramanth leaves, discarding any tough stems, and place them in a large pot.

2 Add the onion, stock, beef, shallots, thyme, chili and crabmeat. Cover and simmer until the meat is tender.

3 Add the okra and cook for a further 8 minutes, then blend the soup in a food processor. Reheat, adding salt and plenty of freshly ground black pepper to taste. Top with croutons.

CELERY

BOTANICAL NAME: *Apium graveolens var. dulce*

FAMILY: *Apiaceae*

Celery is a distinctive vegetable famous for its culinary uses worldwide. It is a relatively tall plant with long stems which grow up vertically, the stem or leaf stalk being the part of the vegetable which is commonly used. The stronger-tasting young leaves are also used in cooking, but to a lesser extent.

Celery has been used for thousands of years as a food source and also for ceremonial rituals. It has been said that garlands found in the tomb of the pharaoh Tutankhamun (died 1323 BC) contained celery. There are also references to the vegetable in ancient Greece and in many other ancient cultures.

There are a range of cultivars available to gardeners, many of which differ from the wild species. Celery is widely used in soups, salads, as a cooked vegetable or as a garnish.

Celery, like peanuts, can provoke a severe allergy. The allergen contained in it does not reduce with cooking so any foods containing celery should be clearly marked.

HEALTH BENEFITS: Celery has been linked to pain relief and reduction in blood pressure and, being low in calories and high in fiber, it is a great food for anyone on a weight-loss regime.

41

WALDORF SALAD

½ cup mayonnaise

1 tbsp white sugar

1 tsp lemon juice

3 apples, cored and chopped

1 cup celery, sliced

½ cup walnuts, halved

½ cup grapes, sliced

Salt and pepper

Serves 6

1 Select a medium-sized bowl and add the mayonnaise, sugar, lemon juice and seasoning to it.

2 Stir in the apples, celery, walnuts and grapes. Chill in the refrigerator, then serve.

CELERIAC GREENS

BOTANICAL NAME: *Apium graveolens rapaceum*
FAMILY: *Apiaceae*

Celeriac, which is closely related to the common leaf celery, is generally used as a root vegetable and the green tops are most often discarded. Often, in supermarkets, the tops are already removed, so it's worth sourcing celeriac from markets or particularly farmers' markets where the whole vegetable is sold intact.

Celeriac which is a member of the carrot family, is often referred to as turnip-rooted celery or simply root celery. These days

it is widely cultivated throughout the world, although its origins lie in the Mediterranean region.

Its use stretches back to ancient Greece and Rome. The root part of the plant is edible raw or cooked and tastes similar to celery. It can be cooked in a variety of ways, which includes steaming, stewing, roasting or adding to soups and stews. The green tops, however, can be cooked as you would other greens or they can be used as a garnish or added to soups, stir-fries, salads and stews.

Celeriac leaves are also most attractive to look at, besides smelling and tasting delicious, so it is a good idea to use them whenever possible.

HEALTH BENEFITS: Celeriac is loaded with vitamins C, B6 and K and is rich in minerals such as magnesium, manganese, potassium, copper and phosphorus. It is useful for those on low-calorie diets for it is very low in calories and high in dietary fiber. There has been research to suggest that celeriac contains certain compounds which are anti-cancer and can be of help to Alzheimer patients.

Celeriac, like peanuts, can can cause severe allergy in some. Moreover, the allergen contained in it does not reduce with cooking, so any foods containing celeriac must be clearly marked.

GREEK SALAD GARNISHED WITH CELERIAC GREENS

DRESSING:

6 tbsp olive oil

1½ tbsp fresh lemon juice

1 tbsp red wine vinegar

2 cloves garlic, finely chopped

1 tsp dried oregano

Salt and pepper

SALAD:

1 head of lettuce

6 small tomatoes, halved

1 English cucumber, sliced

1 medium red onion, sliced

¾ cup kalamata olives, pitted

¾ cup feta cheese

A handful of celeriac greens

Serves 6

1. Whisk all the dressing ingredients together.

2. Combine all the salad ingredients with the dressing and seasonings. Sprinkle over the cubed feta cheese and the celeriac greens and serve.

ASPARAGUS

BOTANICAL NAME: *Asparagus officinalis*

FAMILY: *Asparagaceae*

Asparagus is an herbaceous, perennial plant native to most of Europe, North Africa and western Asia where it is widely cultivated as a crop.

Asparagus produces stout stems (spears) with much-branched, leathery foliage, the leaves being needle-like cladodes (modified stems). Only the youngest and most tender shoots are commonly eaten as they quickly become tough and woody once the buds begin to open.

Asparagus can be prepared in a number of ways, but it is typically eaten as an appetizer or vegetable dish. It can be canned or frozen to make it available out of season. Asparagus has been used as a vegetable and in medicine since ancient times, and can be seen pictured as an offering on an Egyptian frieze dating to 3000 BC.

It was widely used in ancient Greece, Syria and Spain and formed a regular part of the Romans' diet.

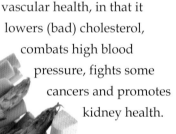

HEALTH BENEFITS: Asparagus is a great source of vitamins, minerals and dietary fiber, together with vitamins A, B complex, folate, C, K and glutathione (antioxidant). Asparagus is useful for cardio-vascular health, in that it lowers (bad) cholesterol, combats high blood pressure, fights some cancers and promotes kidney health.

ASPARAGUS WITH PARMESAN CHEESE (right)

Serves 4

1 lb fresh asparagus spears,
 trimmed
1 tbsp olive oil
¾ cup grated Parmesan cheese
Salt and pepper

1 Preheat the broiler (or barbecue) to a high heat. Lightly coat the asparagus in the olive oil (or they can be left dry), seasoning them well with salt and pepper.

2 Broil or grill for 2–3 minutes or to the desired tenderness. Remove to a plate and sprinkle with grated Parmesan cheese, adding more seasoning if necessary.

ASPARAGUS RISOTTO

(opposite)

Serves 2

1 tbsp olive oil
1 shallot, finely chopped
1 stick celery, finely chopped
1 clove garlic, crushed
¾ cup risotto rice (e.g. Carnaroli or
 Arborio)

½ pint dry white wine
3 cups hot chicken or vegetable
 stock
6 asparagus spears, blanched,
 chopped into discs with the tips
 left whole
1 tbsp unsalted butter
½ cup grated Parmesan cheese
Salt and freshly ground black
 pepper

1 Heat the olive oil in a skillet and gently fry the shallot, celery and garlic until soft but not coloured.

2 Add the rice and fry for one minute, stirring frequently, until thoroughly coated in the oil. Add the wine and simmer until fully absorbed into the rice.

3 Add the hot vegetable stock, a ladleful at a time, stirring between each addition to allow the liquid to become completely absorbed. Continue to do this until the rice is cooked and all the stock has been absorbed.

4 Add the asparagus, butter and Parmesan, season to taste with salt and freshly ground black pepper, and stir well.

5 Serve with a drizzle of olive oil, a scattering of lemon zest and extra grated parmesan to sprinkle on (optional).

MALABAR SPINACH

BOTANICAL NAME: *Basella alba*
FAMILY: *Basellaceae*

Commonly known as pul, vine spinach, red vine spinach, creeping spinach and buffalo spinach, etc., Malabar spinach is a perennial vine in the Basellaceae family, widely used in tropical locations as a leaf vegetable. Originally native to the Indian subcontinent, it is now cultivated in many other tropical regions.

Malabar spinach is a mucilaginous vegetable, indicating that it can be used to thicken soups and stir-fries. It is

something of an acquired taste, being very similar to ordinary spinach (*Spinacea oleracea*) but somewhat stronger-tasting. Contrary to its name, however, Malabar spinach is not related to ordinary spinach.

Common Malabar spinach has oval-shaped leaves with green stems, but there are certain cultivars with red and purplish stems.

HEALTH BENEFITS: Malabar spinach is high in vitamins A and C and loaded with minerals such as iron and calcium. It is low in calories but high in protein and fiber. It also contains good amounts of many B-complex vitamins such as folate, vitamin B6 (pyridoxine), and riboflavin. It is thought to help prevent osteoporosis, iron-deficiency anemia and helps to protect the body from cardiovascular disease and some cancers.

CURRIED MALABAR SPINACH SOUP

1 large potato, peeled and chopped
6 tbsp olive oil
½ cup scallions, chopped
12 cups washed Malabar spinach
⅓ cup all-purpose flour
2 tsp curry powder
4 cups chicken or vegetable stock
1 tbsp lemon juice
1 (8oz) carton non-fat sour cream
Salt and pepper

Serves 6

1 Place the potato in a small pot with water to cover. Bring to a boil, then cook until tender. Drain and set aside.

2 Heat 2 tablespoonfuls of olive oil in a large pot. Add the scallions and cook until tender. Add the cooked potato to the pot, then gradually add the Malabar spinach a little at a time. Add the stock, bring to a boil and cook until the Malabar spinach is tender. Transfer to a food

processor and blend the mixture until smooth. Place in a large bowl and set aside.

3 Heat 4 tablespoonfuls of olive oil in the same pot, that has been rinsed out, and whisk in the flour and curry powder until there are no lumps. Then return the spinach mixture to the pot, along with the lemon juice, stirring well to blend thoroughly.

4 Put the sour cream into a medium bowl, then pour about one cupful of the hot soup onto it and mix well. Stir this cream mixture back into the soup and reheat, but do not allow to boil. Serve the soup immediately garnished with croutons.

BEET GREENS

BOTANICAL NAME: *Beta vulgaris*
FAMILY: *Chenopodiaceae (Amaranthaceae)*

The beetroot, also known as the beet, table beet or golden beet, refers to *Beta vulgaris*, which is a cultivated plant grown for its edible taproots, and which can be found all over the world.

The deep red roots of the beetroot can be prepared for eating in a variety of ways: they can be boiled, roasted, grilled or grated raw, while in eastern Europe, beet soup or borscht is a popular traditional dish. The leaves can also be eaten, usually boiled or steamed and, once cooked, have a similar taste and appearance as cooked spinach.

Beetroot is rich in nutrients and antioxidants. Betanin is the chemical present in beetroot which gives it its deep red colour, and which is used industrially as a food colorant to improve the appearance of tomato pastes, sauces, jams, sweets etc.

HEALTH BENEFITS: Of benefit to pregnant women (reduces risk of birth defects), lowers (bad) cholesterol, reduces risk of colon cancer, boosts liver and kidney function and strengthens the immune system. Rich in vitamins A, C, some B, calcium, iron, phosphorous, manganese, potassium, zinc, betacyanins with antioxidant properties.

SPICY GARLIC BEET GREENS

Serves 2

1¼ lbs beet greens with stems removed
1 tbsp olive oil
2 cloves garlic, finely chopped
¼ tsp crushed chili pepper flakes
Salt and pepper
Lemon wedges to garnish

1 Bring to a boil a large pot of salted water. Add the beet greens and cook them, uncovered, until tender. Drain and blanch immediately in ice water for several minutes until cold. This will stop the cooking process. Drain well and coarsely chop.

2 Heat the olive oil in a large skillet over a medium heat. Add the garlic and pepper flakes. Cook for about a minute, then stir in the greens and sauté them lightly until heated through. Serve with lemon wedges.

CHARD

Botanical name: *Beta vulgaris cicla, B. vugaris flavescens*
Family: *Amaranthaceae*

Chard is a leafy green vegetable widely used throughout the Mediterranean region. There are many different cultivars which vary widely in color. The leaf blade can be green or red in color and the stalks may also vary. Chard is credited with being one of the healthiest vegetables available, and both chard and beetroot are descendants of the wild sea beet *(Beta vulgaris maritime)*. Both have a long history dating back to ancient Greece where they were used medicinally.

Chard comes in a variety of types. The green stalk chard is known as Lucullus, the red stalk Charlotte, or rhubarb chard, and the multi-color stalks are known as bright lights.

Chard can be used in salads when young and boiled or sautéd when mature. Generally, the leaves are harvested at various stages of maturity depending on the type of recipe involved.

Health benefits: Chard is an excellent source of vitamins C, E and K and B6. It is also rich in fiber, chlorophyll and carotenes. It is loaded with important minerals such as magnesium, potassium, manganese, and iron. For a vegetable, it is relatively high in protein and also rich in calcium thiamine, selenium, zinc, niacin and folic acid, nutrients which combine to provide one of the most powerful anti-cancer vegetables in existence.

CHARD & GRUYÈRE QUICHE

Home-made or store-bought
 shortcrust pastry
1 lb chard (or spinach)
Salt
1 medium onion, chopped
1 clove garlic, crushed
2 tbsp olive oil
6 large eggs
½ pt heavy cream
4 oz Gruyère cheese, grated
1 tbsp chopped chervil

Serves 6

1 Preheat the oven to 180C.
Line a deep 9-inch flan tin with
pastry. Chill in the refrigerator for
30 minutes.

2 Slice the chard leaves and stems
and blanch them in boiling, salted
water for 1 minute. Drain and
press out as much liquid as
possible. Cook the onion and
garlic in the olive oil until soft but
do not color. Cool. Beat the eggs
with the cream and season well.

3 Mix the cooled onion mixture,
cheese, chervil and chard into the
custard and pour into the
prepared pastry case. Bake in the
preheated oven for 40–50 minutes.

Serve hot or cold accompanied by
a green salad.

BORAGE

BOTANICAL NAME: *Borago officinalis*
FAMILY: *Boraginaceae*

Borage, commonly known as the starflower, is an annual herb native to the Mediterranean but which has naturalized in many other parts of the world, where it grows satisfactorily, reappearing from year to year by means of self-seeding and spreading prolifically.

Both the leaves and the vivid blue flowers are edible. The plant grows to a height of 2–3.3 feet, and both stems and leaves are hairy, the leaves being alternate and simple. In temperate climates, such as that of the Britain, the flowering season is relatively long, from June to September, while in milder climates, blooming continues for most of the year.

Borage is commonly used as a vegetable in Germany, in the Spanish regions of Aragon and Navarra, on the Greek island of Crete and in Liguria, a region of Italy. Although often used in soups, one of the better known German borage recipes is the green sauce (*grüne sosse*) popular in Frankfurt. In Liguria, borage is commonly used as a filling for the traditional pastas known as ravioli and pansoti, sometimes dressed with a fresh walnut sauce.

HEALTH BENEFITS: Contains vitamins A, B, omega-6 fatty acids, iron, calcium, potassium, manganese, copper, zinc and magnesium. The flowers and oils are mainly used for therapeutic purposes, the oil recommended for arthritis, dermatitis, premenstrual tension (PMT), eczema, diabetes and many other chronic conditions. The flowers are a useful treatment for fevers, coughs and depression.

BORAGE & CUCUMBER DIP

3 large English cucumbers

½ pint sour cream

2 tbsp rice vinegar

½ tsp celery seed

¼ cup scallions, chopped

¼ cup finely chopped young,
  fresh borage leaves

Squeeze of lemon juice

Salt and pepper

Serves 8

1 Slice the cucumbers finely, having first removed the skins.

2 Sprinkle the cucumber with a little salt and set it aside for around 30 minutes. Drain and pat dry with paper towels.

3 Lightly mix all the other ingredients with the cucumber.

4 Garnish with borage flowers (edible) or dill fronds.

MUSTARD GREENS

BOTANICAL NAME: *Brassica juncea*
FAMILY: *Brassicaceae*

Originating in the Himalayan region of India, mustard greens, also known as Indian mustard, Chinese mustard and leaf mustard, is a species belonging to the mustard family and its use as a vegetable dates back some 5,000 years. There are also some subvarieties such as the southern giant curled mustard, which resembles a headless cabbage.

Originally, mustard greens were consumed by many cultures throughout the world, commonly African, Indian, Nepalese, Pakistani, Chinese and Japanese. Today, however, they are used all over the world, including the Americas and Europe.

Mustard greens are some of the healthiest vegetables in existence, and their attractive, peppery flavor gives quite a punch to any dish to which they are added. Visually, it is an attractive vegetable, some of the leaves being a rich emerald green in color, while others can be shades of deep red or purple.

There are many ways to cook mustard greens and while it is a personal preference, it is best not to over-cook them as their nutritional content may become compromised. They can also be served raw, and are a great addition to any salad. They are also delicious added to pasta dishes.

HEALTH BENEFITS: Mustard greens are very healthy, in that they possess antioxidant and anti-inflammatory properties known to detoxify the body. They are loaded with vitamins A, C, E, K with many important minerals besides. Mustard greens help to protect the cardiovascular system and have anti-cancer properties too.

LEFT & OPPOSITE: Mustard greens come in both curly and flat-leaved varieties.

1 In a large pot, sauté the garlic in the olive oil and cook for about a minute without letting it brown.

2 Add the mustard greens and stock and cook until the greens are just about wilted. Toss in the sesame oil, season and serve.

Serve as a vegetable side dish or with rice as a main dish.

SAUTÉED GARLIC & MUSTARD GREENS

2 cloves garlic, finely chopped
1 tbsp olive oil
1 lb mustard greens, washed and torn into large pieces
3 tbsp vegetable stock
¼ tsp dark sesame oil
Salt and pepper

MUSTARD CABBAGE

BOTANICAL NAME: *Brassica juncea rugosa*

FAMILY: *Brassicaceae*

Mustard cabbage, which is in the same family as mustard greens, is also known as cabbage leaf mustard, broad-leaved mustard, heading mustard and heart mustard. A member of the Brassica family, it is native to central Asia, and has been used in Far Eastern cuisines for centuries.

While it is still widely used in Asia, it is more of a rarity in many Western countries, but it can be found in specialist Asian food stores, where it can be bought fresh or pickled.

Mustard cabbage is undoubtedly an acquired taste, being very strong-tasting and pungent, so much so that it cannot be eaten raw, but with its distinctive mustard flavor it is sometimes added to soups and stews. As a pickle, mustard cabbage is a common addition to many Asian tables. It is prepared in a similar way to sauerkraut, and can be served as a side dish with a variety of Asian meals.

HEALTH BENEFITS: Pickling tends to degrade many of the nutrients, although pickled mustard cabbage still contains vitamins A, B6, and K, while other nutrients, such as calcium, folate, iron, manganese, magnesium potassium, niacin and riboflavin are also present. It has been used in herbal medicine for centuries for conditions such as diabetes and it is said to lower (bad) cholesterol.

SALTY PICKLED MUSTARD CABBAGE

½ lb mustard cabbage

¾ cup cider vinegar

¾ cup water

¾ cup sugar

½ a red chili, finely chopped.

1½ tbsp salt

1 Cut the mustard cabbage into 1–2-inch pieces and put into a large jar. Combine the remaining ingredients, making sure all the sugar is dissolved. Pour over the cabbage, making sure it is completely covered.

2 Cover the jar and refrigerate. Consume within 1 week.

BROCCOLI

BOTANICAL NAME: *Brassica oleracea var. italica*

FAMILY: *Brassicaceae*

Broccoli is a member of the cabbage family, whose large flower heads are used at a vegetable that can be eaten raw or cooked. It is a cultivar group of the species *Brassica oleracea*. The flower heads are green in color and sprout, tree-like, from a thick edible stalk. It is related to the cauliflower, which it closely resembles apart from the flowers being green in color rather than white.

As a cultivar, broccoli was first developed in the northern Mediterranean by the Italians, although its popularity soon spread to Europe and to the United States by way of Italian immigrants.

Broccoli is rich in vitamins and minerals and is a good source of dietary fiber. There are three varieties of broccoli: calabrese, sprouting and romanesco.

HEALTH BENEFITS: Contains multiple nutrients thought to have potent anti-cancer properties, including diindolymethane and selenium. Helps to develop a healthy nervous system, promotes muscle growth, may help to regulate blood pressure. Good for osteoporosis, skin damage, the eyes, heart and diabetes. Loaded with vitamins A, B6 and folate and vitamins C, K and E, together with minerals including phosphorus, potassium and magnesium.

BROCCOLI & CAULIFLOWER GRATIN

8 oz broccoli

7 oz cauliflower

1 oz butter

1 oz flour

½ pint milk

3 oz breadcrumbs

2 oz Cheddar cheese, grated

Salt and pepper

Pinch of grated nutmeg

Serves 4 as a side dish

1 Parboil the broccoli and cauliflower until almost tender.

2 To make the white sauce, melt the butter, stir in the flour and add the milk, whisking constantly. Season with salt, pepper and nutmeg.

3 Mix the vegetables with the sauce, then top with the breadcrumbs and cheese. Bake at 350F for 20 minutes. (To make the gratin extra cheesy, sprinkle a little Parmesan over the top of the dish before serving.)

COLLARD GREENS

BOTANICAL NAME: *Brassica oleracea acephala, B. oleracea viridis*
FAMILY: *Brassicaceae*

Collard greens are loose-leafed cultivars of *Brassica oleracea*. Collards are grown for their large, dark-colored leaves which, when cooked, are bursting with flavor. The cultivar group name is Acephala, which means 'without a head' in Greek, indicating that the plant does not have a close-knit head like a cabbage. Although collards originated in eastern Europe or Asia, they seem to grow better in colder climates.

Popular cultivars include Blue Max, Georgia Southern, Butter collard and Champion. Collards are related to kale and spring greens, which are very similar genetically as well as in texture and appearance. They are gown commercially and are popular for their slightly bitter-tasting edible leaves. They are available all year-round but are of better quality and more nutritious during the winter months.

Collards are also used as ornamental garden plants and look most attractive in winter, grown in containers and baskets.

HEALTH BENEFITS: Collards are regarded as a healthy food, in that they are a good source of fiber as well as being rich in vitamins A and C, together with other nutrients with anti-cancer properties.

Collards are also of benefit to Alzheimer's sufferers, being rich in many vital B-complex groups of vitamins, such as B3, B5, B6 and riboflavin. They also contain folates, iron, calcium manganese, selenium, copper and zinc.

COLLARD GREENS WITH BACON

1 lb collard greens, cut into pieces, thick ribs removed

4 slices thick-cut bacon, chopped

1 onion, thinly sliced

Pinch chili flakes

3 cloves garlic, minced

2 cups chicken stock

Squeeze of lemon juice

Salt and black pepper

Serves 4 as a side dish

1 Cook the bacon in a large skillet until crisp. Transfer to a plate, leaving the bacon fat behind.

2 Add the onion, chili flakes and garlic to the same skillet and sauté until translucent. Add the collard greens, pour in the chicken stock and bring to a boil. Reduce to a simmer, then cook the greens, covered, until tender. Return the bacon to the pan, add the lemon juice and season to taste.

KALE

BOTANICAL NAME: *Brassica oleracea acephala, B. oleracea viridis*
FAMILY: *Brassicaceae*

Kale, also known as borecole, is a vegetable in the Brassica family. Its leaves grow from the center, without forming a head, like the cabbage, and are frilly in texture. Kale is closely related to other Brassicas, such as broccoli and cauliflower but is in the same cultivar group known as Acephala, with spring greens and collard greens being other members of that group.

The name borecole derives from the Dutch word, *boerenkool*, which means famer's cabbage. Kale was eaten by the ancient Greeks and the Romans and by the Middle Ages, was commonly consumed all over Europe.

Today, there are many different cultivars. Kale is available for most of the year, but as with other Brassicas is better during the winter months. It is highly perishable, and should be stored in the refrigerator and consumed as soon as possible after purchase.

There are many different ways to prepare kale. It lends itself to many Asian dishes, especially when combined with soy sauce, red chili pepper flakes or peanuts.

In Ireland, kale is combined with mashed potatoes to make the famous traditional dish known as Colcannon, while in Portugal it is added to soups, and in Italy and Germany to stews, while in the southern United States it is often served braised or mixed with other greens, such as collards. Flavored kale chips can also be made and used as an alternative to potato chips. Kale also has an ornamental use as an attractive garden plant.

HEALTH BENEFITS: Along with other Brassicas, kale is extremely healthy to eat besides being very low in calories. It is rich in beta carotene, vitamins C and K, as well as in calcium and iron. It is reputed to have potent anti-cancer properties and is said to lower (bad) cholesterol. It is an antioxidant, anti-inflammatory and is good for liver health.

CREAMY PEA & KALE SOUP

½ lb kale

1 tbsp butter

1 large onion, chopped

1 medium potato, sliced

2 cloves garlic, finely chopped

2 cups frozen peas (thawed)

2 cups milk

½ cup chopped parsley

Salt and pepper

Serves 4

1 Wash the kale and chop the leaves into small pieces, retaining the tougher stems. Melt the butter and add the chopped kale stems, onion and potato slices. Cook over a medium heat for about 10 minutes until the potato is soft and the onion translucent. Add the garlic and kale leaves and stir. Cover the pot and cook on a low heat to allow the kale to steam for about 5 minutes. Remove from the heat and stir.

2 Blend the peas with the kale in a food processor until the mixture is smooth, adding the milk slowly as required. Add the parsley and blend again. Return the purée to the pot and gently reheat. Season well with salt and pepper and serve.

KALE CHIPS

½ lb kale
1 tbsp olive oil
1 tsp salt

1 Preheat the oven to 350F. Line a sheet pan with parchment paper.

2 Using a knife or kitchen shears, carefully remove the leaves from the thick stems and tear them into bite-sized pieces. Wash and thoroughly dry the kale in a salad spinner. Place the kale on the sheet pan, drizzle with olive oil and sprinkle with salt.

3 Bake until the edges of the kale are brown but are not burnt (about 10 to 15 minutes).

CHINESE BROCCOLI

BOTANICAL NAME: *Brassica oleracea alboglabra*

FAMILY: *Brassicaceae*

Also known as Chinese kale, mustard orchid or flowering kale, Chinese broccoli is a handsome leaf vegetable with glossy, blue-green leaves. The stems are relatively thick and similar to those of regular broccoli but with smaller flower heads. The Cantonese name for Chinese broccoli is Kai Lan or Gai Lan, so it may be known under either of these names in Asian foodstores.

Related to broccoli, Chinese broccoli is very similar in taste, although it is stronger in flavour with a slightly mustard-tasting finish. It is also related to other brassicas such as Brussels sprouts, cabbage, kale and cauliflower. It is commonly used not only in Cantonese cooking but also throughout China. Generally is it is used in stir-fries, combined with garlic, ginger and oyster sauce and is a favourite with dumplings.

It is generally thought that Chinese broccoli originated from cabbage seeds brought to the Far East by the Portuguese, and over many generations became the vegetable we know today. As with many brassicas, Chinese broccoli is a cool-season crop, best reserved for winter use.

HEALTH BENEFITS: Chinese broccoli has been used in traditional Chinese medicine for centuries to combat many disorders. Like its Western counterpart, it is loaded with nutrients, vitamins and minerals, being particularly high in calcium, and is considered to be as good a source of the mineral as milk. It also contains copper, folate, manganese, potassium, riboflavin, phosphorus, thiamin and zinc. Vitamins include A, B6, C, E and K, and it is also known to possess considerable anti-cancer fighting properties.

CHINESE BROCCOLI IN OYSTER SAUCE

1½ lbs Chinese broccoli

1 tbsp peanut oil

2 tbsp oyster sauce

1 tsp seasame oil

½ tsp salt

Serves 4 as a side dish

In a wok, stir-fry the Chinese broccoli in the peanut oil until it turns bright green (3–4 minutes). Add the oyster sauce, salt and sesame oil, heat through and serve.

GREEN CABBAGE

BOTANICAL NAME: *Brassica oleracea capitata*

FAMILY: *Brassicaceae*

Cabbages are one of the most commonly grown vegetable plants in general use throughout the world. They are biennials that are usually grown as annuals. Cabbages are large, round, leafy members of the Brassica family, of which there are many varieties harvested at different times throughout the year. The green cabbage is the most common and is the most often grown, being one of the most commercially successful varieties.

Its rapid growth, resistance to frosts and long storage possibilities means that the green cabbage is grown all over the world. Not only is it economically versatile, but it is inexpensive, packed with goodness, and has become a vegetable staple for many cultures. It can be eaten raw or cooked and in countries such as Germany is often pickled and served as *sauerkraut*, an important traditional dish.

It is difficult to trace the exact history of this cabbage, but it was most likely domesticated somewhere in Europe before 1000 BC, and by the Middle Ages had become an important part of European cuisine.

Through the centuries, the word 'cabbage' has been used as slang for numerous items, occupations and activities. Both cash and tobacco have been described as cabbage, while 'cabbage-head' refers to a fool or stupid person and 'cabbaged' means exhausted, or more vulgarly, in a vegetative state.

HEALTH BENEFITS: Good for constipation, stomach ulcers, headache, slimming, skin disorders, eczema, jaundice, scurvy, rheumatism, arthritis, gout, eye and heart disease. Contains vitamin C (antioxidant), B complex and folate, vitamin K, glucosinolate and minerals.

FRESH SAUERKRAUT SALAD

1 tbsp olive oil

1 medium onion, thinly sliced

1 medium cabbage

1¼ cups cider vinegar

½ cup apple cider

½ cup water

1 tbsp of salt

Chopped chives to garnish

1 Heat the oil in a large pot set over a medium heat. Sauté the onion, stirring constantly, until it is soft and transluscent.

2 Add the cabbage, vinegar, cider, water and salt and bring to a boil.

3 Cover and simmer for 30–45 minutes until the cabbage is tender (adding more water, if necessary, to stop the mixture from completely drying out).

4 Store the sauerkraut in a refrigerator and consume within 2 weeks. Serve with a selection of charcuterie or cold meats.

SAVOY CABBAGE

Botanical name: *Brassica oleracea capitata sabauda*

Family: *Brassicaceae*

The Savoy cabbage is a comparatively recent addition to the Brassica family, having been developed in the 16th century, when it was first cultivated on the Italian, Swiss and French borders by the Duchy of Savoy. Other names for the Savoy include cole, curly cabbage, Lombardy or Milan cabbage.

The Savoy is a relatively weighty cabbage for its size, and with its distinctive, ruffled, crinkly leaves is visually most attractive. The peak season for the Savoy cabbage, as with other Brassicas, runs from November through April when it is at its best. At this time it should be unblemished, bright and fresh and should ideally be eaten straight away, its shelf life being somewhat shorter than that of the green cabbage.

Despite its rough, textured appearance the Savoy is a very tender and sweet-tasting cabbage, making it a great choice for salads or for use as wraps. Unlike some of the other cabbage varieties, the Savoy does not emit the sulfur-like odor during cooking, which reinforces its popularity to a great extent.

HEALTH BENEFITS: The Savoy cabbage provides fiber, vitamins A, C, K and B6, folate, potassium, manganese, thiamin, calcium, iron and magnesium. Like other cabbages, it is of high nutritional value, and its antioxidant qualities recommend it for helping to combat a variety of diseases.

STUFFED SAVOY CABBAGE WITH TOMATO SAUCE

1–2 large Savoy cabbages

1½ oz lard (a light olive oil may be
 substituted)

1 large onion, chopped

2 tbsp paprika

3 lb 4 oz minced pork

1 lb cooked Basmati rice

Salt and freshly ground black
 pepper

1 chicken bouillon cube

14 oz chopped canned tomatoes

1 tbsp tomato purée

1 tbsp sugar

Serves approx. 10

1 Put the whole cabbages in a large pot, add sufficient freshly boiled water to cover, and boil for 5-10 minutes, or until the outer leaves can easily be pulled out. Remove the cabbages from the pot and leave to cool slightly, then separate out the leaves and set aside to drain and cool completely. Keep the cooking water.

2 Heat the lard or oil in a skillet and add the chopped onion, sautéing it over a medium heat until soft but not brown. Tip the cooked onions into a bowl and stir in the paprika, followed by the minced pork and the rice. Season with salt and freshly ground black pepper and mix well.

3 Take a cabbage leaf and cut away a little of the tough central stalk to make it easier to roll. Add a spoonful of the pork mixture to the stalk end of the leaf, then roll it into a sausage shape, tucking in the ends as you go. (Try to roll the leaf as firmly as possible to prevent it from unrolling during cooking.) Repeat with the remaining cabbage leaves until you have used up all the stuffing mixture. Shred any leftover cabbage and use it to line the bottom of a large pot. Place the stuffed leaves in the pot as snugly as possible, with the joins underneath, then cover with any remaining shredded cabbage.

4 Stir the bouillon cube into the reserved cooking water, stirring until dissolved. Use this to cover the cabbage rolls, bring to a boil, then reduce the heat and simmer gently for 1–1½ hours, covered, until the pork is cooked (the pork is cooked when the cabbage rolls run clear when tested with a skewer). During cooking, check the liquid levels, adding more boiling water if needed to prevent the pot from boiling dry.

5 Tip the tomatoes into a small pot, add the tomato purée and sugar. Fill the tomato can with cold water and stir it into the pot. Season well. Bring the sauce to a gentle simmer and cook for 25 minutes, stirring occasionally, until thick. Remove from the heat and leave to stand.

6 Arrange the cooked cabbage leaves on a preheated serving dish and cover them with the tomato sauce. Add a little sour cream if it is to your taste.

BRUSSELS SPROUT

BOTANICAL NAME: *Brassica oleracea gemmifera*
FAMILY: *Brassicaceae*

The Brussels sprout is a cultivar in the Gemmifera group of cabbages. Botanically, sprouts belong to the same family as cabbages, collard greens, broccoli and kale. They are grown for their edible buds which resemble miniature cabbages in appearance. It is not know where the Brussels sprout originated, although it has always been popular in Brussels, Belgium, where similar cultivars were known since Roman times. The Brussels sprout we know today was first written about in 13th-century Belgium with its popularity spreading thereafter to other parts of Northern Europe. Production of Brussels sprouts in the United States began in the 18th century, when French settlers brought them to Louisiana.

Like most Brassicas, the Brussels sprout is a winter

vegetable which flourishes in cold weather. When fresh, sprouts have a delicate flavor but when over-cooked an unpleasant sulfur-like odor is emitted. They can be cooked by boiling, microwaving or steaming and used in much the same way as other Brassicas.

Health benefits: Brussels sprouts, especially when eaten raw, contain excellent levels of vitamins C and K, with more moderate amounts of B vitamins, such as folic acid and vitamin B6; essential minerals and dietary fiber also exist in lesser amounts.

BRUSSELS SPROUTS WITH BACON

2 lbs Brussels sprouts
¼ cup olive oil
1 cup finely chopped bacon
1 tbsp Dijon mustard
Salt and pepper

Serves 4 as a side dish

1 Bring a pot of water to a boil and blanch the Brussels for about 1 minute. Transfer them to a bowl filled with ice water. Leave the sprouts to cool, then drain onto paper towels.

2 In a large skillet, cook the bacon in the olive oil over a moderate heat until crisp. Transfer the bacon onto a plate. Add the sprouts to the skillet, adding the mustard when they begin to brown. (Add a little water if the mixture starts to stick.) Transfer to a serving dish, sprinkling the bacon over the top.

KOHLRABI TOPS

BOTANICAL NAME: *Brassica oleracea gongylodes*
FAMILY: *Brassicaceae*

Kohlrabi, also known as German turnip or turnip cabbage, is a low-growing, stout cultivar in the cabbage family. The name derives from the German word for cabbage (*kohl*) and the word *rabi*, which is a Swiss/German variant for turnip.

It originated in Northern Europe although it is most popular in Eastern and Central Europe. It is also eaten in north India and Kashmir where it is often served with rice.

Kohlrabi was created through artificial selection, which is quite surprising, and with its distinctive swollen stem is now very different from its wild cabbage (*Brassica oleracea*) relative. Kohlrabi stems are similar in taste to those of broccoli, but milder and sweeter. When young, the stems are crispy and juicy and are tender enough to be eaten raw in salads or slaws as well as cooked.

Kohlrabi, when bought, usually comes with the leaves still on. The leaves sprout from the stem and are dark green and firm. When raw, the leaves are tough, sharp and quite bitter to taste and are never eaten. When cooked, however, they become quite mild and taste very like broccoli. The leaves are also similar to those of kale or collard greens and are interchangeable.

HEALTH BENEFITS: Kohlrabi tops are highly nutritious, containing dietary fiber and anticancer properties, B-complex vitamins, vitamins A and K and minerals such as copper, potassium, manganese, iron and phosphorus. Kohlrabi tops are extremely low in calories and are therefore ideal for those on weight-reducing regimes.

CREAM OF KOHLRABI SOUP

2 tbsp butter

3 tbsp butter

1 onion, chopped

1 celery stalk, chopped

8 cups chopped kohlrabi tops

3 cups vegetable stock

3 tbsp all-purpose flour

2 cups milk

Salt and pepper

Chopped parsley to garnish

Serves 4–6

1 In a medium pot, melt the 2 tablespoonfuls of butter and sauté the onion and celery until tender. Add the kohlrabi and stock and simmer for 10 minutes.

2 Using a food processor, purée the soup, following the manufacturer's instructions, then pour the soup into a clean pot.

(Alternatively, a stick blender may be used in the same pot to process the soup.)

3 In a small saucepan, over a medium heat, melt the 3 tablespoonfuls of butter, stir in the flour and add the milk. Stir until thickened, then add to the soup. Gently reheat, season with salt and pepper and serve, garnished with a little chopped parsley.

TURNIP GREENS

BOTANICAL NAME: *Brassica rapa*
FAMILY: *Brassicaceae*

The turnip, also called the white turnip, or neep in Scotland and the north of England, is usually consumed as a root vegetable, although the leaves, called turnip greens or tops, may be eaten, too.

The turnip thrives in temperate climates. It is a native of Eurasia, where it has been cultivated for centuries, and was even known to the ancient Greeks and Romans.

Turnips belong to the Brassica family of plants, which includes cabbage, kale and Brussels sprouts, and have many characteristics in common.

Today, the small, tender varieties are usually consumed by humans, being less bitter and healthier to eat than the bulbous root, while the larger ones are often grown specifically as animal feed.

Supermarkets, unfortunately, often remove the valuable green tops from the turnips before they are displayed, but it is still possible to buy the vegetables intact if you shop around or attend farmers' markets or whole food specialists.

Turnip greens are commonly seen in south-eastern United States' cooking, traditionally eaten during the fall.

HEALTH BENEFITS: Turnips are low in calories, high in antioxidants, minerals and dietary fiber. The greens are packed with vitamins A, C, K, B-complex vitamins, carotenoid, xanthin and lutein, while valuable minerals include copper, calcium, iron and manganese.

103

ORECCHIETTE WITH TURNIP GREENS

Serves 4

1¼ lbs dried orecchiette (little ears
 pasta)
1–2 tbsp olive oil
4–5 salted anchovies
1 clove garlic, crushed
Dried red chili flakes (according to
 taste)
1¼ lbs turnip greens (*cima di rapa*),
 well-washed and with stems
 removed
Pecorino cheese, grated or
 in slivers (use a vegetable peeler)

1 Cook the orecchiette in a large
pot of boiling, salted water,
according to the package
instructions, until al dente.

2 Meanwhile, heat the oil in
another large pot and sauté the
anchovies, garlic and chili flakes
for 2–3 minutes without browning
them. Then add the turnip greens
and cook for a further 3–4
minutes, or until the turnip greens
are tender and wilted. Season well
with sea salt and black pepper.

3 Drain the orecchiette and add to
the pot with the turnip greens,
mixing well to coat. Spoon onto
plates and serve with a little
pecorino cheese sprinkled over.

BOK CHOY

Botanical name: *Brassica rapa chinensis*
Family: *Brassicaceae*

Bok choy or *Brassica chinensis* is related to the cabbage but bears little resemblance to the Western cabbage we know and love. Chinensis varieties do not form heads; instead, they have smooth, dark-green leaf blades forming clusters reminiscent of mustard or celery.

The Chinese commonly refer to bok choy as pak choy or the white vegetable.

Bok choy has been cultivated in China since the fifth century and is widely used throughout Asia, where it is a staple of Asian cooking, found in stir-fries, appetizers and main dishes. It is known for its sweet, succulent and nutritious stems.

Like many Asian vegetables, however, its use in the West is relatively recent, having been introduced to North America and Europe in the 1800s. Bok choy is now commonly found in markets throughout the world, catering both to the Chinese diaspora and to northern markets which appreciate its resistance to cold.

HEALTH BENEFITS: Bok choy is of benefit to the eyesight, teeth, bone density, stomach ulcers, immune system, sluggish intestinal tract, lowers the risk of heart disease and blood pressure and has anticancer properties. Bok choy is rich in vitamins C, A, K, B-complex, calcium, manganese, iron, potassium and phosphorous.

CHICKEN & BOK CHOY STIR-FRY

1 tbsp peanut oil

4 6-oz boneless chicken breasts, cut into bite-size pieces

4 heads baby bok choy, cut into quarters lengthwise

¼ cup soy sauce. (Use low salt soy sauce if preferred)

1 tbsp rice wine

¼ cup barbecue sauce

Salt and pepper

Serves 2 (together with steamed rice)

1 Heat the oil in a large wok or skillet over a medium to high heat. Season the chicken with pepper. (Do not over-salt as there is plenty in the soy and barbecue sauces.) Turn the chicken regularly, turning until golden brown and cooked through. Transfer to a plate.

2 Add the bok choy and a little water to the wok. Cover and cook for about 2–4 minutes until the bok choy is tender.

3 In a medium-sized bowl, mix the soy sauce, rice wine and barbecue sauce together. Add to the wok and bring to a boil. Return the chicken to the wok and cook, tossing, until it is thoroughly heated through.

NAPA CABBAGE

Botanical name: *Brassica rapa pekinensis*
Family: *Brassicaceae*

The napa cabbage, Chinese cabbage or celery cabbage is a hardy biennial, usually grown as an annual, which is related to the Western cabbage and is in the same family as the turnip. Other than the ambiguous term 'Chinese cabbage,' the most widely used names for Chinese cabbage in North America is bok choy, literally 'white vegetable,' from the Cantonese, or pak choi (choy).

Napa cabbages are sweet, crunchy and celery-flavored and are equally good raw or cooked.

Pekinensis cabbages have broad green leaves with white petioles, tightly wrapped into cylindrical formations and usually forming compact heads. As the group name indicates, this vegetable is particularly popular in northern China around the capital city of Beijing (Peking). It has been cultivated for food in China for thousands of years and has also been used in Chinese medicine for a similar period.

In China the napa cabbage has become a sign of prosperity and its image often appears as a symbol in glass and on porcelain.

Health benefits: Of benefit to the eyesight, teeth, bone density, stomach ulcers, immune system, sluggish intestinal tract, lowers the risk of heart disease, lowers blood pressure and has anticancer properties. The napa cabbage is very low in calories making it ideal for those on weight-loss diets. It is high in vitamins C, K and calcium, potassium, phosphorous, manganese, magnesium and iron.

NAPA CABBAGE SALAD

1 napa cabbage, shredded

1 carrot, grated

½ cup sweetcorn

1 apple, core removed and sliced

1 tsp fresh minced ginger

1 tbsp sesame oil

6 tbsp cider vinegar

1 tps fine white sugar.

1 tbsp finely chopped
 coriander/cilantro

Serves 4–6

1 Make a dressing by combining
the oil, vinegar, ginger and sugar
in a large bowl. Stir until the sugar
is dissolved.

2 Add all the other ingredients to
the dressing and toss well.
Garnish with the chopped
coriander.

TATSOI

BOTANICAL NAME: *Brassica rapa narinosa*

FAMILY: *Brassicaceae*

Tatsoi, also known as rosette bok choy, spoon mustard, spinach mustard, is an Asian, cool-season variety of *Brassica rapa* grown for greens. It has been used in China and Japan for centuries. In Chinese its name is *wu ta cai* and in Japan it is called *tasai*.

The plant has dark-green leaves and, as one of its names suggests, forms thick rosettes. It is a low-growing plant.

Tatsoi has a distinctive flavor and is very tender to eat. Although it can be bought in North America and Europe, it is more likely to be found in specialist stores and farmers' markets rather than in mainstream supermarkets.

Tatsoi is a useful vegetable, good as an alternative to spinach, arugula or watercress. Like arugula it has a tangy, peppery taste which complements vegetable, fish, shellfish and meat dishes well and is good dressed with soy sauce. Tatsoi is commonly found included in salad mixes.

HEALTH BENEFITS: Like bok choy and other Asian brassicas, tatsoi is of benefit to the eyesight, teeth, bone density, stomach ulcers, immune system, sluggish intestinal tract, lowers the risk of heart disease, lowers blood pressure and has anticancer properties. Tatsoi is rich in vitamins C, A, K, B-complex, calcium, manganese, iron, potassium and phosphorous.

CRANBERRY, WALNUT & FETA SALAD WITH TATSOI, ARUGULA & DIJON MUSTARD DRESSING

1 cup walnuts, roughly chopped

1 cup dried cranberries

1 cup feta cheese, crumbled

4 cups washed tatsoi leaves

4 cups mixed arugula, curly
 endive and frisée leaves (washed)

Sprigs of mint to garnish

DRESSING:

1 tbsp Dijon mustard

2 tbsp olive oil

1 tbsp white wine vinegar

Salt and pepper

Serves 2

1 Combine the walnuts, cranberries and salad leaves together (not the feta and mint).

2 Combine all the ingredients for the dressing, whisking them well together. Pour over the salad, lightly coating all the ingredients. Sprinkle over the feta and garnish with the mint.

116

KOMATSUNA

BOTANICAL NAME: *Brassica rapa perviridis, B. komatsuna*
FAMILY: *Brassicaceae*

Komatsuna, a Chinese cabbage, is also known as Japanese mustard spinach or Korean greens. The leaves of the komatsuna are dark green with slender stalks. It is most often grown in the spring and autumn being intolerant of extremes of temperature. It is a fast-growing vegetable, however, that is ready for harvesting in 35 days after sowing, particularly if the weather is fair.

It is widely used in Japan, Taiwan and Korea, added to stir-fries, soups and salads, or it can be boiled or even pickled. Being more closely related to turnips than to the other leafy brassicas, it has a slightly sweet-sour taste and is very tender like raw spinach. It is interchangeable with bok choy, chard and spinach.

HEALTH BENEFITS: Komatsuna is loaded with vitamins C, E, A, K besides having many important minerals. Komatsuna greens help to protect the cardiovascular system. It is rich in iron and is reputed to protect against cancer.

JAPANESE UDON NOODLE & SHRIMP WITH KOMATSUNA LEAVES

1 tbsp sesame oil

4 cloves garlic, crushed

12 large frozen shrimps, thoroughly thawed out

4 cups chicken or vegetable stock

2 tbsp Thai fish sauce

1 tbsp soy sauce

1 tbsp sriracha or other hot sauce

2 packs ready-to-use udon noodles

2 big handfuls komatsuna leaves

Squeeze of lime juice to serve

1 tbsp toasted sesame seeds

Serves 4

1 Heat the sesame oil in a large wok, add the garlic and fry very gently.

2 Add the shrimp and cook briefly until the color changes. Remove from the wok to avoid over-cooking.

3 Add the stock, fish sauce, soy sauce and sriracha sauce, then add the udon noodles and heat through.

4 Return the shrimp to the soup, along with the komatsuna leaves, and heat until the leaves begin to wilt.

5 Arrange the ingredients in small bowls and serve with a squeeze of lime and sprinkling of toasted sesame seeds.

GREEN TEA

BOTANICAL NAME: *Camellia sinensis*
FAMILY: *Theaceae*

All types of tea (green, black and oolong) are produced from the *Camellia sinensis* plant using different methods. Fresh leaves from the plant are steamed to produce green tea, ensuring that they undergo minimal oxidation during processing.

The concept of green tea originated in China but has since developed associations with many cultures throughout Asia. In more recent times it has become more popular in the West, where black tea has more traditionally been consumed. Today, tea is the most widely drunk beverage in the world, second only to water.

Green tea has become the raw material for extracts which are used in various beverages, health foods, dietary supplements and cosmetics items, and many varieties have been developed in the countries where it is grown, varieties which can differ substantially from one another due to the various conditions under which they have been grown and processed.

Green tea has been the subject of many scientific and medical studies, over the last few decades, to determine the efficacy of its legendary health benefits, with some evidence suggesting that regular drinkers of the substance may develop a lower risk of heart disease and certain types of cancer.

Steeping is the process by which tea becomes a drink, also referred to as brewing. The container or teapot, in which the leaves are steeped, should first be warmed so that the tea does not cool down before there is time to drink it.

HEALTH BENEFITS: Tea helps weight loss, stomach problems, vomiting, osteoporosis, diarrhea, headaches, cancers, Crohn's disease, Parkinson's disease and cardiovascular disease. It lowers (bad) cholesterol and prevents chronic fatigue syndrome (CFS), dental cavities, kidney stones, skin damage, stamina and benign prostatiec hyperplasia (BPH).

CHILI PEPPER LEAF

BOTANICAL NAME: *Capsicum frutescens*

FAMILY: *Solanaceae*

The chili pepper is a member of the family Solanaceae which is also known as the nightshade family. It is a native of the Americas but following the discovery of America by Europeans the chili pepper spread throughout the world and is now used in both food and medicine. Chili peppers have been part of the human diet since at least 7500 BC when they were domesticated by the Mexicans.

The spread of the chili pepper to Asia was a result of Portuguese traders who, aware of its value, traded it throughout the region.

The substances that give chili peppers their distinctive, hot intensity when eaten is caused by several chemicals known as *capsaicinoids*. There are many species of capsicums, with different levels of intensity, but while the plants are mainly grown for their fruit, in South-East Asia they are also grown for their leaves which are used for a number of purposes. Pepper leaves are only sold in Asian stores, particularly those selling Filipino, Vietnamese or Korean ingredients. Usually they come dried or frozen.

Pepper leaves must always be cooked, because they are toxic if consumed raw. It is not advisable to grow your own chili plants for their leaves as some cultivars retain their toxicity in their cooked state.

Edible types can be added to stir-fries or eaten as a vegetable. They are mild in flavor, compared with the peppers, but add great color to a dish. They are similar in taste to spinach with a slightly peppery flavor.

HEALTH BENEFITS: Pepper leaf has been used in herbal medicine for centuries. It is reputed to benefit respiratory disease, headaches, arthritis, menstrual problems, ulcers, and lowers cholesterol, blood pressure and blood sugars.

STIR-FRIED VEGETABLES

2 tbsp light soy sauce

2 cloves garlic, minced

1 tsp minced ginger

2 tbsp all-purpose flour

1 cup chicken or vegetable stock

¼ cup cold water

3 tbsp peanut oil

8 oz spinach, well washed

½ cup frozen chili pepper leaves,
 thawed

Serves 2 as a side dish

1 Combine the soy sauce, garlic and ginger in a small bowl, then mix the flour, stock and water in another bowl.

2 Place the wok over a high heat, then add the oil and vegetables, tossing them together with the soy sauce mixture for about 1 minute. Then slowly add the flour mixture and bring to a boil, when the sauce will thicken slightly. Serve.

CURLY ENDIVE & FRISÉE

Botanical name: *Cichorium endivia crispum*

Family: *Asteraceae*

Endive is a type of chicory of which there are several kinds. Curly endive (*Cichorium endivia crispum*) has narrow, green, curly outer leaves, these being quite bitter tasting and coarse in texture.

Curly endive is commonly used in salads throughout the world. In France it is called *chicorée frisée*, where it is a mainstay of salads, or simply chicory in the United States; other names include escarole and cut-leaf endive.

There is some confusion over the terms curly endive and frisée. Both are the same species, but frisée is a smaller and slightly less bitter variety.

Botanically, this herbaceous leafy salad vegetable belongs to the Asteraceae (daisy) family and is closely related to radicchio and Belgian endive. Endive originated in Asia Minor, and there is evidence that it was cultivated by the ancient Greeks and Romans. It is a cool-season crop and consequently grows well in temperate zones.

These days, curly endive and frisée can be found in most stores and supermarkets, although frisée can be a little more illusive. Look for good-quality leaves because discolored, yellow endive is not worth eating at all.

Health benefits: Endive is very low in calories, making it great for weight-watchers. It is a source of vitamins A, C, E, K and B-complex, as well as carotene and folic acid, and contains valuable minerals such as manganese, potassium, iron and copper. It is thought to be of benefit to those with high blood pressure, gallstones and respiratory problems, and is also beneficial to the metabolism and the skin.

ENDIVE SALAD WITH BACON & CROUTONS

2 washed heads of endive

2 tbsp red wine vinegar

Salt and pepper

6 oz thickly sliced bacon, cut into lardons

Slices of French baguette, cut into croutons

Serves 4

1 Roughly tear the endive leaves into bite-size pieces, placing them in a large salad bowl.

2 Spread the croutons out onto a sheet pan, placing them in a hot oven to toast. Sauté the bacon lardons in their own fat until crisp, remove, then scatter the bacon over the salad, keeping the pan with the bacon fat for later.

3 Turn off the heat and deglaze the pan containing the bacon fat with the vinegar, then pour the warm vinaigrette over the salad. Add the croutons and toss gently.

TIP: A hot poached egg, placed on the salad at the last minute, makes a delicious addition.

CATALOGNA

BOTANICAL NAME: *Cichorium intybus catalogna*
FAMILY: *Asteraceae*

Catalogna is a type of chicory native to Asia, North Africa and Europe, with a history dating back to Roman times. There are many cultivars of the chicory plant, Catalogna being one of them. It is a plant whose leaves and long stalks resemble those of dandelions.

The plant has always been popular in the Mediterranean and is widely used in Italy. It is becoming available in other countries, but it may be necessary to search for it in specialist stores or farmers' markets, etc. While it can be used in salads, it is quite bitter and is often served cooked.

HEALTH BENEFITS: Used in herbal medicine for centuries, Catalogna, like other chicory species, has many health benefits. It it known to benefit the digestive system, alleviating constipation and indigestion. It is of benefit to the liver, gallstones, the cardiovascular system and aids weight-loss, arthritis and gout. It contains vitamins A, B-complex C, E and K, including carotene and folic acid, and is a good source of minerals such as manganese, potassium, iron and copper.

COOKED CATALOGNA

A less bitter, deeper flavor results from using this method, even though the crunch is lost.

Sauté the catalogna lightly in a little butter, then add chicken stock and seasoning. Cover and braise for 20 minutes or until the liquid is all but gone. Good with Parmesan or an anchovy sauce.

RADICCHIO

Botanical name: *Cichorium intybus rubifolium*
Family: *Asteraceae*

Radicchio, also known as Italian chicory, red endive or red chicory, is a fast-growing perennial treated as a leaf vegetable. Unusually, it has red leaves with white veins fanning out from its base. It is spicy and bitter in taste, and has been used in salads in Italy for centuries.

Different cultivars are named after Veneto cities, with Chioggia being a variety with compact beet-red, bitter leaves, while Treviso is less pungent and has long, conical, compactly-arranged leaves. Castlefranco is a hybrid between radicchio and endive and is also mild. Lastly, Veron has red, open leaves with white veins.

Despite being in the Asteraceae (daisy) family, Radicchio resembles a small cabbage. It is at its best in autumn and winter, although it is freely available in supermarkets all-year-round. In Italy, it is often brushed with olive oil and then grilled or used as an ingredient in risottos. It is also perfect for a winter salad and often paired with citrus fruits, pears, apples and root vegetables, such as carrots.

Health benefits: Radicchio is a good source of dietary fiber, vitamins and minerals, and has phytonutrients and antioxidants. As with other chicory plants, it is very low in calories and therefore a good choice for those on weight-loss diets. It contains selenium, phosphorus, potassium, calcium, vitamins A, C, E, K and B-complex and folate. Known to reduce (bad) cholesterol, it promotes healthy bones, helps regulate blood sugar levels and is good for the eyes and digestive system.

RADICCHIO RISOTTO

1 head radicchio, sliced (save
 some for a garnish)
4 cups chicken or vegetable stock
3 tbsp butter
1 small onion, finely chopped
Salt and pepper
2 cups arborio rice
1 cup dry white wine
¾ cup grated Parmesan cheese
½ cup mascarpone

Serves 4–6

1 In a medium pot, bring the stock
to a boil, then reduce the heat,
maintaining a simmer. In a
separate pot over a medium heat,
melt the butter, add the onion,
season with salt and pepper, and
cook, stirring occasionally, until
tender. Add the radicchio and
cook, stirring occasionally, until it
is wilted and tender.

2 Add the arborio rice and stir,
ensuring that each grain of rice is
coated with butter. Add the white
wine and cook, stirring, until the
liquid is absorbed. Add 1 cup of
the stock and cook, stirring, until
the liquid is absorbed. Repeat the
process with a second and
subsequent cups of stock until the
rice is tender (about 20 minutes).

3 Stir in the mascarpone, and most
of the Parmesan, reserving some
to sprinkle over at the end. Serve
immediately, garnished with a few
sliced radicchio leaves.

BELGIAN ENDIVE

Botanical name: *Cichorium intybus witlof*
Family: *Asteraceae*

Belgian endive, also known as Dutch witloof ('white leaf') is a relatively new cultivar with a small head of creamy-colored leaves. Although it is not well-documented, Belgian endive is thought to have been developed by accident in Belgium in the 19th century.

The vegetable is grown underground or indoors without light, cultivated below the soil surface, with only the leaf tips showing.

This prevents the leaves from becoming green or opening up, while the blanching process stops the leaves from becoming bitter and coarse, making Belgian endive one of the mildest and most delicate in flavor of all the chicories.

Today, France is the world's largest producer. Although called 'endive,' Belgian endive must not be confused with true endive, (*Cichorium endivia*), which is a different type. Today, Belgian endive is a supermarket staple so it is easily found, but avoid heads which have become discolored or wilted. It can be cooked, baked, boiled or eaten raw.

Health benefits: Belgian endive is known to stimulate the digestive system and detoxify the liver. It has antioxidant and antiviral properties and is good for the immune system. It has respectable amounts of vitamins and is high in folate, beta-carotene, iron and phosphorous. It is good for regulating blood sugar levels and is reputed to lower (bad) cholesterol. It is also an effective laxative.

BELGIAN ENDIVE BAKED WITH CHEESE

4 heads Belgian endive
1 tbsp olive oil
Salt and pepper
1 tbsp butter
1 tbsp all-purpose flour
¾ cup milk
Pinch ground nutmeg
½ cup Gruyère cheese, grated
Parsley to garnish

Serves 4

1 Thoroughly clean the Belgian endive, removing any coarse or discoloured leaves. Cut each head in half lengthways.

2 Line up the halves in a large, heavy skillet. Add ¼ cup of water and the olive oil, season with salt and pepper, then cover the skillet and bring to a boil over a high heat. Reduce the heat and simmer until the endive is very tender when pierced with a skewer (10–20 minutes). Uncover and cook for about 5–10 minutes over a medium heat, turning the heads occasionally until the liquid evaporates and the endive is a light golden brown.

3 In a small saucepan, melt the butter on a gentle heat. Add the flour and blend well, then add the milk and the nutmeg, stirring constantly until the sauce thickens. Stir in half the cheese.

4 Arrange the endive in a single layer in a shallow oven dish, spooning the sauce over the top. Sprinkle the top evenly with the remaining cheese.

5 Bake, uncovered, in a hot oven until the sauce is bubbling and the top lightly browned. Garnish with parsley leaves.

JUTE LEAF

Botanical name: *Corchorus olitorius*
Family: *Sparrmanniaceae*

Jute leaves, also known as jute mallow, bush okra, Egyptian spinach, mallow or okra leaves, are the green growth from one of the varieties of jute plants that produce edible leaves used as a vegetable or food ingredient.

Jute belongs to the genus Corchorus, and is widely found in tropical and subtropical regions from Asia to Africa and now worldwide, although it is thought to have originated in India. Jute leaves are used in cuisines all over the Middle East, Africa, the Far East and Central America.

Jute is a hardy plant which can be grown easily and is well-known to be resistant to pests. It is a tall plant reaching 12 feet in height. It is highly valued for its strong fiber and nutritious leaves, which resemble spinach or samphire, when cooked, and form a slimy syrup similar to okra. This is not to everyones liking, and is something of an acquired taste. Jute leaf is rarely found fresh in Western supermarkets, but it can be found frozen in some specialist stores.

HEALTH BENEFITS: Jute leaves are rich in vitamins A, B6, C and E. Minerals include iron, manganese, magnesium, niacin, potassium, thiamin, zinc and copper. It is of benefit to arthritis, headaches, stomach aches, liver problems, diabetes and heart disease, the eyesight and skin and is thought to have anticancer properties.

EGYPTIAN JUTE SOUP (MOLOKHIA)

1 lb frozen jute leaves
4 cups vegetable stock
½ onion, finely chopped
2 cloves garlic, minced
½ tsp ground cumin seeds
½ tsp ground cardamon
½ tsp ground coriander
2 tbsp olive oil
Juice of 1 lemon
Croutons

Serves 4

1 Defrost the frozen jute leaves thoroughly, then drain off any excess fluid and finely chop.

2 Bring the stock to a simmer and stir in the jute leaves. Leave to simmer for about 20 minutes.

3 In another small saucepan, set over a low heat, combine the onion, garlic, spices and oil for a few minutes until the onion and garlic are golden – do not allow to brown or burn. Stir the mixture into the soup. Add the lemon juice and serve with the croutons.

CORIANDER/CILANTRO

Botanical name: *Coriandrum sativum*
Family: *Apiaceae*

Coriander, also known as Chinese or Mexican parsley, cilantro or dhania, in the Indian subcontinent, is an annual herb (leaves) and spice (seeds) in the Apiaceae family and is related to the carrot. Cilantro, not to be confused with culantro (*Eryngium foetidum)*, which is a close relative, is the Spanish word for coriander, also deriving from coriandrum. It is the common term in North America for coriander leaves due to the influence of Mexican cuisine.

Coriander is native to a large part of southern Europe, North Africa and Asia. The leaves taste differently from the seeds, which have pleasant citrus overtones, and indeed the Chinese believed that coriander seeds had the power to bestow immortality. The leaves, however, are something of an acquired taste, the flavor having been compared to the smell emitted by stink bugs, and similar chemical groups are involved (aldehydes). Once converted, however, its fans would be loath to do without it.

Coriander seeds, like many spices, contain antioxidants which can delay or prevent the spoilage of food, while both the leaves and the seeds have been found to contain antioxidant and antibacterial properties although the leave were found to exert a stronger effect.

Coriander has been used as a folk medicine for the relief of anxiety and insomnia, and in traditional Indian medicine as a diuretic by boiling equal amounts of coriander seeds and cumin seeds, then cooling and consuming the resulting liquid. In holistic and traditional medicine, it is used to relieve flatulence and as an aid to digestion. It has also been documented as a traditional treatment for type 2 diabetes.

HEALTH BENEFITS: Antibacterial, digestive, anti-inflammatory, useful for urinary tract infections, nausea, flatulence, for regulating blood sugars, lowering cholesterol, and freshening breath. Contains vitamins B complex, C, carotene (antioxidant), calcium, phosphorus, iron and oxalic acid.

CORIANDER/CILANTRO CHUTNEY

2 cups loosely packed cilantro
 leaves

½ cup loosely packed mint leaves

½ cup chopped onion

½ a hot green chili (seeds
 removed)

1 clove garlic, chopped

1 tbsp fresh lime juice

1 tsp sugar

¼ tsp salt

¼ tsp ground cumin

Combine all the ingredients in a
food processor and blend until the
mixture is almost smooth. Serve
within 2 hours as an
accompaniment to Indian food.

PICO DE GALLO

Use this salsa or chutney to add interest to sandwiches, cold meats, baked potatoes or grilled fish.

3 tbsp finely chopped red onion
2 cloves garlic, finely chopped
2 large ripe tomatoes, peeled,
 seeds removed and chopped
2 hot Serrano or Jalapeño peppers,
 finely chopped
3 tbsp chopped coriander/cilantro
2 tbsp lime juice
Salt and pepper

Serves 4

1 Combine the onion and the garlic; pour 2 cups of boiling water over them, then drain thoroughly. Discard the water and allow to ingredients to cool.

2 Combine all the ingredients together. Refrigerate for 2 hours and serve.

SEA KALE

BOTANICAL NAME: *Crambe maritima*
FAMILY: *Brassicaceae*

Sea kale, also called crambe, coming from the Greek word for cabbage, is a flowering plant in the Brassicaceae family. It grows wild along the shores of Europe, and is commonly found growing above the high tide mark on shingle beaches. It has now spread further afield, however, and has become naturalized along the coasts of California and Oregon as well as in other areas.

There is evidence that its use dates back to ancient Greece, although it has been cultivated as a garden vegetable since the 1600s. The asparagus-like shoots are served, usually steamed, and seasoned with salt and pepper. It can also be eaten raw, in salads or baked in the oven.

Young shoots should be harvested when they are four or five inches long, crisp and tender, and it should retain its firmness when correctly cooked. It has a subtle flavor, rather like hazelnuts, with a slight bitterness about it.

Sea kale is often overlooked, but nowadays is becoming increasingly more popular, being a small shrub that grows well in saline soils. As well as a vegetable, it is also used as an ornamental plant in gardens.

HEALTH BENEFITS: Sea kale has diuretic properties, boosts the immune system, is high in vitamin C and benefits the endocrine system. Sea kale is rich in carbohydrates, making it suitable for sports enthusiasts who need instant energy or those needing to gain weight for health reasons.

SEA KALE WITH BUTTER SAUCE

4 oz sea kale
1 small onion, finely chopped
3 tbsp white wine vinegar
8 oz unsalted butter, cubed
Juice of 1 lemon
Salt and pepper

Serves 2

1 Place the onion into a pot with the vineger and 3 tbsp water.

2 Bring to a boil and reduce the liquid to about 2 tablespoonfuls.

3 Reduce the heat and gradually whisk in the butter, one piece at a time, until the sauce is smooth, thick and glossy. Add the lemon juice.

4 Steam the sea kale for 3–4 minutes, ideally in an asparagus kettle. Arrange on a warm serving dish, season, and spoon over the butter sauce.

CARROT TOPS

Botanical name: *Daucus carota sativus*

Family: *Apiaceae*

The carrot is a ubiquitous, usually orange, root vegetable that is eaten throughout the world. The wild ancestor of the carrot is likely to have come from Iran or Afghanistan, where there is a naturally occurring subspecies of the wild carrot. Over the centuries, however, carrots have been selectively bred to improve their taste and texture and there are a great number of varieties from which to choose. While they are usually orange, they also come in a range of colors, including white, red, purple and yellow. Carrots were first cultivated for their leaves and seeds rather than their roots, but close relatives of the carrot, such as fennel, dill and cumin are still grown for their seeds.

Carrot tops are probably the most under-utilized of all the greens available in our shops today and, in many cases, they have had their tops removed before they even arrive. Increasingly, however, carrots can more often be obtained with their tops intact and, providing they are fresh enough, these can be used as a green vegetable in their own right.

Carrot leaves can be added to soups and stews or, if tender enough, can be briefly sautéed, while in moderate amounts, being quite bitter and coarse in texture, they can be added to salads. Use only the leaves as the stems are too stringy and fibrous.

HEALTH BENEFITS: Carrot tops are rich in potassium, calcium, magnesium, vitamin K and protein. Potassium is a key mineral in our bodies, and keeping it at correct levels keeps all our organs in the best possible condition.

CARROT SOUP

2 large potatoes, peeled and
 chopped
1 large onion, quartered
4 large carrots
Chicken or vegetable stock
Salt and pepper

Serves 6

1 Place all the ingredients in a
stock pot and cover them by about
2 inches with the stock. Cook until
the potatoes and carrots are soft
(about 20 minutes), then purée
everything in a food processor.

2 Reheat briefly, and serve with
plenty of freshly ground black
pepper, some crusty bread, and a
spoonful or two of carrot-top
pesto (see below).

CARROT-TOP PESTO

1 cup lightly packed carrot leaves
 (stems removed)
6 tbsp extra-virgin olive oil
1 large garlic clove
Pinch of salt

3 tbsp pine nuts, lightly toasted in
a dry skillet
¼ cup freshly grated Parmesan
 cheese

In a food processor, combine the
carrot leaves, oil, garlic and salt

and process until finely minced.
Add the pine nuts and pulse until
finely chopped. Add the Parmesan
and pulse just until combined.
Taste and adjust the seasoning.
Use immediately, or cover and
refrigerate for up to 2 days.

ARUGULA

BOTANICAL NAME: *Eruca sativa*
FAMILY: *Brassicaceae*

Arugula has many common names, including rocket, roquette, rucola, rucoli and Italian cress. Arugula is in the Brassicaceae family and is a widely used salad vegetable native to the Mediterranean region, it being a small, low-growing annual herb with dandelion-like leaves.

Arugula is famous for its pungent, peppery flavor and is very strong-tasting for a leafy green. Its use dates back to Roman times when it was considered to be an aphrodisiac, and it was banned later on, in the Middle Ages, for this very reason, although it is now innocently enjoyed as a salad vegetable.

Arugula has become naturalized all over the world and can even be gathered from the wild. It is an easy plant to grow at home and is often mixed with other salad greens such as mesclun. In Italy it commonly accompanies pasta and pizza dishes and in Ischia, an island off the coast of Naples, Italy, it is made into a liqueur called *rocolino*.

Today, arugula has become something of an everyday salad vegetable, and is often found in stores and supermarkets bagged up, washed and ready to eat.

HEALTH BENEFITS: Arugula is rich in antioxidants and is a good source of folic acid. It contains vitamins A, C and K as well as minerals such as iron, magnesium, manganese, potassium, phosphorus, riboflavin, thiamin and zinc. Of benefit to the gallbladder, liver and stomach.

PEAR, POMEGRANATE, BLUE CHEESE & ARUGULA SALAD

2 pears, cored and sliced

2 bunches arugula, torn

A handful of radicchio leaves

3½ oz blue cheese

3 oz shelled walnuts

¼ cup pomegranate seeds

Serves 4

Arrange the salad ingredients in an attractive fashion on individual plates and serve with the salad dressing of your choice.

FENNEL

BOTANICAL NAME: Foeniculum vulgare

FAMILY: *Apiaceae (Umbelliferae)*

Fennel is a hardy, perennial, umbelliferous herb, with yellow flowers and feathery leaves. It is indigenous to the shores of the Mediterranean but has become widely naturalized in many parts of the world, especially on dry soils near sea coasts and on river banks. It is also commonly found along roadsides or in pastures.

Fennel propogates itself very successfully, often far from its usual habitat, and can be considered by some to be an invasive weed.

Fennel is a highly aromatic and flavorful herb with important culinary and medicinal uses and, along with the similar-tasting anise, is one of the three main ingredients of absinthe.

Fennel is cultivated all over the world for its strongly-flavored leaves and seeds, its foliage being similar in flavor to that of dill. In India the leaves are used as a leafy garnish and cooked either on their own or with other vegetables, while they are used in a special kind of omelet, called *ijjeh*, in Syria and Lebanon. Dried or fresh fennel leaves are also known to complement fish dishes.

In Roman times, fennel was considered to be good for the eyesight and even today, in India, it is still credited with this property. It is also considered to be beneficial for sufferers from high blood pressure, for the digestive system, and is an effective diuretic.

HEATH BENEFITS: Useful properties include vitamins A, B complex, C, E, iron, copper, zinc, phosphorous, manganese, selenium, magnesium, potassium, calcium and antioxidants.

CHORIZO & FENNEL OMELET

2 tbsp olive oil
½ cup chorizo pieces
1 fennel bulb, finely sliced
4 free-range eggs, lightly mixed
 together
Salt and pepper
Fennel leaves, chopped

Serves 2

1 Heat 1 tbsp olive oil in a large skillet and sauté the chorizo over a medium heat until it is slightly browned.

Remove, then add the sliced fennel bulb, sautéing it until it is soft but not browned. Remove and place with the chorizo to one side.

2 Clean the skillet with paper towels, then add a little more oil and set it on the heat. Season the eggs well with salt and pepper and add them to the skillet (they will immediately start bubbling).

3 Lift the cooked edges of the omelet with a spatula and tilt the pan so that the uncooked egg runs beneath the lifted edge. Repeat the process around the skillet for about 1 minute or until no liquid egg remains, but do not overcook.

4 Distribute the cooked chorizo and fennel evenly over the omelet, then fold it in half and transfer it to a hot plate. Serve garnished with cherry tomatoes and chopped fennel leaves.

WATER SPINACH

BOTANICAL NAME: *Ipomoea aquatica*
FAMILY: *Convolvulaceae*

Water spinach is a fast-growing, semi-aquatic, tropical plant grown as a vegetable. It is known by a variety of names, besides water spinach, such as river spinach, Chinese morning glory, swamp cabbage and kangkong.

Water spinach, as the name suggests, grows best in water or on very moist soil. It is propagated by cuttings taken from the stem shoots that root along nodes on the stem, or it can also be raised from seed. It is commonly grown all over South-East Asia, but is extensively used as a comestible in Thailand Burma (Myanmar), Cambodia, Malaysia, Vietnam and China.

Its precise origin is not known but it is throught to have come originally from China or India. It is possible for it to be grown in more temperate climates, and does well grown in containers placed in sunny locations and kept well-watered.

The tasty stems are used in stir-fries to give an added crunch, where they are combined with chili, garlic, ginger and other flavorings.

The leaves can be used as a salad ingredient, but are rather stringy in texture.

Water spinach is not usually available in the USA and Europe, but it can be found in some specialist Asian foodstores.

In some sub-tropical parts of the United States, such as Florida, water spinach has been naturalized, and unfortunately to the detriment of the surrounding environment, causing it to be termed a noxious weed and an invasive species.

Health benefits: Studies show that water spinach may be beneficial for diabetes and it is considered to be good for the eyes, the memory, the digestion, some infections and the liver. Water spinach is rich in antioxidants, which help protect the body from disease. It contains vitamins C, B6 and K and many important minerals such as calcium, copper, magnesium , folate, phosphorus and zinc.

STIR-FRIED WATER SPINACH

1 tbsp peanut oil

1 large clove of garlic, sliced

½ tsp sugar

2 lbs water spinach, trimmed, with
 the stems cut into 2-inch pieces

1 cup cashew nuts

2 tbsp soy sauce

Black pepper

Serves 4 as a side dish

1 Heat the peanut oil in a large non-stick skillet over abmedium-high heat. Add the sliced garlic and stir-fry for 30 seconds or until golden. Do not allow the garlic to burn.

2 Add the sugar, the water spinach and cashew nuts to pan. Stir-fry for 3 minutes or so until the spinach wilts. Add the soy sauce and stir-fry 1 minute more.

3 Remove from the heat, season well with the pepper and serve.

TAIWAN LETTUCE

BOTANICAL NAME: *Lactuca sativa angustana*

FAMILY: *Asteraceae*

The lettuce is said to have originated in ancient Egypt, where it was first cultivated and in time spread throughout the world.

Lactuca sativa angustana is a Taiwanese variety that is used all over China as a cooked vegetable, usually in stir-fries. It is also known as Chinese lettuce, Vietnamese lettuce or Orient sword leaf, and has long, pointed green leaves, both the leaves and the stems being very crisp and tender with a unique flavor.

Taiwan lettuce is a fast-growing variety where the leaves can be picked and used at any stage. It is most often found in Asian foodstores in the USA and Europe.

Health benefits: Like other lettuces, Taiwan lettuce is a good source of vitamins A, B6, K, C and a good source of dietary fiber. It also contains calcium, folate, iron, magnesium, manganese, niacin, phosphorus, potassium, riboflavin and thiamin.

TAIWAN FRIED LETTUCE

2 lbs Taiwan lettuce, cut into lengths (wash only if necessary)
2 tsp Chinese rice wine or dry sherry
2 tsp soy sauce
¾ tsp sugar

1½ tbsp peanut oil
2 garlic cloves, peeled and minced
1½ tsp minced ginger
Good pinch red pepper flakes
½ tsp salt
½ tsp sesame oil

Serves 4–6

1 Combine the rice wine or dry sherry, soy sauce and sugar in a small bowl, stirring well. Set aside.

2 Heat a wok on a medium-high heat and add the oil. When hot, add the garlic, ginger and red pepper flakes. Stir-fry for a few seconds to activate the spices, then add the dry lettuce. Stir-fry the lettuce, sprinkling it with the salt, until the leaves begin to wilt.

3 Give the sauce a quick re-stir and pour it into the wok. Stir-fry for 1–2 more minutes, until the lettuce turns dark green. Remove from the heat and stir in the sesame oil. Serve immediately.

166

BUTTER LETTUCE

Botanical name: *Lactuca sativa capitata*
Family: *Asteraceae*

The butter lettuce is an annual plant in the Asteraceae family. It is commonly produced as a salad vegetable, but can be grown specifically for its seeds.

Lettuce was first cultivated by the ancient Egyptians who developed a common weed into a cultivar and grew it for its seeds, using them to produce oil. There is also evidence that the lettuce was used by the ancient Greeks and Romans. Later in the 16th–18th centuries, however, lettuces were further developed to produce many of the cultivars we know today, and which are used in kitchens throughout the world.

Lettuces can be used in all kinds of salads, and can also be cooked and made into soups. In general, however, it is more usual to consume them raw, the leaves being very delicate, tender and subtle in flavor. The butter lettuce is sometimes known as a cabbage lettuce due to its shape. Butter lettuces come in green and red cultivars as well as dwarf varieties. They are also known as Boston or Bibb lettuce.

Butter, or butterhead lettuces, are sold in practically all mainstream stores and supermarkets throughout the world.

Health benefits: Like other lettuces, butter lettuce is a good source of vitamins A, B6, K, C and is rich in dietary fiber – also calcium, folate, iron, magnesium, manganese, niacin, phosphorus, potassium, riboflavin and thiamin.

169

ASIAN LETTUCE WRAPS WITH CHICKEN FILLING

1 tbsp canola oil

1 tbsp dark sesame oil

1 tbsp rice vinegar

2 tsp soy sauce

½ tsp hot chili-garlic sauce

1 tsp fresh grated ginger

2 garlic cloves, minced

Salt

4 6-oz skinless, boneless chicken
 breasts, halved

Cooking oil spray

8 butter lettuce leaves (about 1
 head)

½ cup julienne-cut carrots

2 scallions, chopped

Serves 4

1 Combine the first 8 ingredients together in a small bowl and whisk together throughly. Reserve 2 tablespoonfuls of this oil mixture for later.

2 Place the remaining oil mixture in a large zip-top plastic bag. Add the chicken breast halves, seal,

and leave to marinate in the refrigerator for 1 hour, turning the bag occasionally. Remove the chicken from the bag and discard the marinade.

3 Heat a large non-stick grill pan over a medium-high heat. Spray the pan with the cooking oil and add the chicken to the pan. Cook for 12 minutes or so until the chicken is cooked through and golden, turning once. Leave to stand for 5 minutes before slicing it.

4 While the chicken is standing, stir-fry the carrots for a few minutes until tender. Divide the chicken evenly between the lettuce leaves, topping each with sliced carrot and chopped scallions and about 1 teaspoonful each of the reserved oil mixture.

ICEBERG LETTUCE

BOTANICAL NAME: *Lactuca sativa*
FAMILY: *Asteraceae*

Until the 1930s the iceberg lettuce was known as the crisphead lettuce. It was first developed in California, in the Salinas Valley, and was shipped all over the United States by train. To keep it fresh, it was packed in ice, hence the name 'iceberg.'

Today's iceberg is as popular as ever, in that it is easy to handle, stays crisp for hours after slicing and is relatively inexpensive to buy; in fact, it has become a staple of fast food outlets worldwide. Even today, with so many more fashionable varieties of salad vegetables available, it has lost none of its popularity.

The iceberg is very similar in appearance to a white cabbage, being similarly dense and compact in its form. Unlike the cabbage, however, the leaves, although large, are very tender and fine.

This is a very crunchy lettuce with a high water content and like all lettuces, its ancestors can be traced back to ancient Egypt where early lettuces were first cultivated. The Egyptians cultivated lettuces for a number of uses, but, interestingly, they believed the lettuce could increase sexual prowess, thus making it sacred to the fertility god Min.

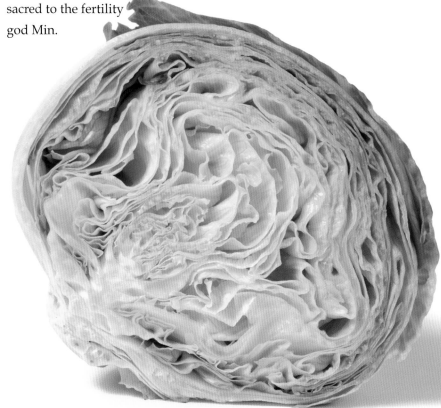

HEALTH BENEFITS: There is a misconception about lettuces that their food-value is quite low, which is far from the truth. Icebergs are a good source of vitamins A and C, and contain fiber, iron, potassium and calcium. They are useful for those watching their waistlines, being very low in calories.

172

ICEBERG WEDGES, BACON & BLUE CHEESE

¾ cup mayonnaise

¼ cup fat-free evaporated milk

1 tbsp lemon juice

1 head iceberg lettuce

2 bacon slices, cooked and
 crumbled

1½ cups halved grape tomatoes

6 oz blue cheese

Serves 6

1 Combine the first 3 ingredients together in a small bowl.

2 Remove the outer leaves from the lettuce and discard. Rinse under cold running water, draining well. Remove core and slice the lettuce into 6 wedges.

3 Top each lettuce wedge, set on an individual plate, with ¼ cup of the dressing, some bacon pieces and tomato halves. Sprinkle generously with the crumbled blue cheese and serve.

CRESS

Botanical name: *Lepidium sativum*

Family: *Brassicaceae*

Sometimes referred to as garden cress to distinguish it from similar plants also referred to as cress, *Lepidium sativum* is a cool-season, fast-growing edible annual. It is sometimes called pepper grass, due its peppery flavor, and is also known as poor man's pepper and pepperwort. The word cress comes from the old Germanic word *cresso*, which means sharp or spicy.

The plant has naturalized in many countries, but is said to have originated in Iran. Garden cress is very easy to grow, being suitable for growing outdoors, indoors, in containers and in hydroponic systems. Edible shoots can be harvested in 1–2 weeks after planting.

The seeds from cress have been used since ancient times in the traditional medicine of India and in Europe. For culinary purposes, it is usually seen in sandwiches, soups, salads and as a garnish due to its attractive appearance.

Health benefits: Garden cress is richer in vitamin C than oranges. It also contains vitamin A, which is essential for eye health, and vitamins E and B-complex. It is reputed to be of benefit to the cardiovascular system and is an anti-inflammatory. It is an excellent source of folic acid and iron.

EGG & CRESS OPEN SANDWICHES

2 slices good bread, buttered

2 hard-cooked eggs, sliced

Salt

2 tbsp mayonnaise (optional)

Cress

Serves 1

Spread the mayonnaise over the buttered bread, then add the sliced egg, a little salt, and garden cress.

LEMON BALM

BOTANICAL NAME: *Melissa officinalis*
FAMILY: *Lamiaceae*

Also known as balm or balm mint, and not to be confused with bee balm, which belongs to the genus Monarda. The plant is known to attract bees, hence *melissa*, which is Greek for honey bee.

The plant is native to central southern Europe and the Mediterranean, but is grown all over the world, not only in herb gardens and to attract bees, but also as a crop for use in medicines, cosmetics, and for flavoring food.

The leaves are rough and heavily textured and produce a sweet, lemon-like scent when rubbed between the fingers. They are similar in shape to mint leaves, and indeed lemon balm belongs to the same family, Lamiaceae, as mint.

Lemon balm is often used to flavor ice creams and in herbal teas, both hot and iced, often in combination with other herbs such as spearmint. It is frequently added to fruit dishes and candies, but can be used to enhance fish dishes. It is a key ingredient of lemon balm pesto.

HEALTH BENEFITS: Lemon balm has valuable medicinal properties, for example, as an antispasmodic, antidepressant, for dyspepsia, and to relieve stress and tension. It is useful for sleep disorders such as insomnia and nightmares. Has long been thought to promote longevity.

LEMON BALM TEA

3 tbsp lemon balm leaves
1 slice lemon

1 Use a pestle and mortar to crush the lemon balm leaves.

2 Place the crushed leaves in a small teapot and pour in boiling water on top. Leave to steep for about 8 minutes, then strain and serve with a slice of lemon.

PEPPERMINT

BOTANICAL NAME: *Mentha x piperita*
Family: *Lamiaceae*

Peppermint was first described as a species by Carl Linnaeus in 1753, but it is now universally agreed to be a hybrid cross between spearmint and watermint. The plant is a native of Europe but is now cultivated throughout the world. Both the leaves and flowering tops are utilized, best collected as soon as they can be dried. The wild form of the plant is less suitable for this purpose, and cultivated plants usually have better oil content. They may be allowed to lie and wilt a little before distillation, or they may be taken directly to the still.

Peppermint has a long culinary history, with archeological evidence dating its use back thousands of years. Peppermint has a high menthol content and it is widely used in teas and tisanes and for flavoring confectionery, chewing gum and toothpaste.

Menthol is known to activate cold-sensitive receptors in the skin, causing the cooling sensation that follows its topical application; this is why it is used in some shampoos, soaps and skin care products. The essential oil is also used in aromatherapy.

HEALTH BENEFITS: Peppermint treats gastronintestinal problems, heartburn, nausea, flatulence, liver and gall bladder problems. It is applied topically for headaches, muscle pain, toothache, mouth inflammation, skin conditions and as a mosquito repellant.

PEPPERMINT TEA

3 tbsp peppermint leaves
1 small teapot full of hot water

1 Use a pestle and mortar to crush the peppermint leaves.

2 Place the crushed leaves in a small teapot and pour boiling water on top. Leave to steep for about 8 minutes, then strain and serve.

WATERCRESS

Botanical name: *Nasturtium officinale*
Family: *Brassicaceae*

Watercress is a perennial plant that grows in aquatic or semi-aquatic conditions. It is a native of Europe and Asia, and is a member of the Brassicaceae family, making it a relative of mustard, radish and garden cress that are all well-known for their peppery flavor. Watercress is the most ancient of the leafy vegetables and there is evidence that it was grown by the ancient Greeks, Romans and Persians.

Watercress has a creeping habit, and bears very small, white flowers; the leaves become progressively more bitter to the taste as they appear.

It frequently grows around the headwaters of chalk streams but can also be cultivated hydroponically on a commercial scale, making it available virtually all-year-round.

Because it is relatively rich in vitamin C, watercress was suggested (among other plants) by English military surgeon John Woodall (1570–1643) as a remedy for scurvy. It is a natural companion to strongly flavored meats such as game and makes a delicious soup as well.

Health benefits: An antioxidant, watercress is useful for respiratory problems, anemia, hair loss, flu, as a laxative, a diuretic, and as an aphrodisiac. Stimulates the metabolism. Used topically for arthritis, earache, eczema, warts, and as an antiseptic. Contains significan amounts of iron, calcium, iodine and folic acid in addition to vitamins A and C.

189

WATERCRESS SOUP

2 tbsp butter

2 tbsp olive oil

1 onion, finely chopped

1 clove garlic, finely chopped

3 medium potatoes, peeled and
 thinly sliced

2 cups chicken or vegetable stock

Salt and ground black pepper

2 bunches watercress, very well
 washed and roughly chopped

¾ cup of milk

¼ cup light cream

Serves 2

1 Heat the butter and oil in a large
pot over a medium heat and sauté
the onion and garlic until soft and
translucent (do not brown).

2 Stir in the potatoes and pour in
sufficient stock to just cover them.
Season with salt and black pepper,
cover with a lid, then simmer for
10 minutes or so until the potatoes
are tender.

3 Tip the watercress into the pan
and stir in the milk and remaining
stock. Bring to a boil, then reduce
the heat and simmer, uncovered
for a further 10 minutes.

4 Using a food processor, blend the soup to a smooth consistency, then stir in the cream. Adjust the seasoning to taste and serve, garnished with a few picked watercress leaves.

BASIL

Botanical name: *Ocimum basilicum*

Family: *Lamiaceae*

Basil is a culinary herb of which there are many varieties, such as Thai basil, sweet or Italian basil, lemon basil and holy basil.

Originally from India, where it has been cultivated for thousands of years, its use has now spread worldwide, and it is of particular importance in the cuisines of South-Eeast Asia. In Europe, particularly in Italy, it has become a staple herb due to the wonderful affinity it has with the tomato.

While most common varieties of basil are treated as annuals, some are perennial in warm, tropical climates, including holy basil and a cultivar known as African blue. Depending on the cultivar, the flavor of basil can vary from sweet to pungently strong. Basil is at its best when freshly picked and is generally used in cookery to add flavor at the last minute, for over-cooking can quickly destroy its fine anise flavor.

Health benefits: Basil contains many important essential oils known to have antibacterial and anti-inflammatory properties. It is packed with important nutrients with high levels of beta-carotene, vitamins A, K and other compounds. Of benefit to the skin, eyes and cardio-vascular system, Basil is particularly rich in iron and many other minerals such as potassium, manganese, copper and magnesium. It is also reputed to possess anticancer properties.

CAPRESE SALAD

4 large ripe tomatoes, cut into
 slices
1 lb fresh buffalo mozzarella, cut
to the same thickness as the
 tomatoes
⅓ cup fresh basil leaves
3 tbsp extra virgin olive oil
Fine sea salt
Freshly ground black pepper

On a large plate, alternate the
tomato slices with the mozzarella
and basil leaves so that they
overlap slightly. Drizzle with the
olive oil and season well with sea
salt and black pepper.

PERILLA

BOTANICAL NAME: *Perilla frutescens*
FAMILY: *Lamiaceae*

Perilla, native to East Asia, is a herb belonging to the mint family, Lamiaceae. It is known by several names depending on location, but all are classified under a single species, *Perilla frutescens*. Different varieties of perilla are consumed in Korea, Laos, Vietnam, India and Nepal. Other names for perilla include Chinese basil, Japanese basil, sesame leaf and shiso.

Perilla leaves resemble stinging nettles, but are somewhat rounder.

The plant grows well in temperate climates and is self-sowing. It has become naturalized in much of North America, and is now considered to be an invasive species. This wild version is quite toxic, with only cultivated perilla being safe to eat.

Perilla is a fragrant, leafy herb of which different cultivars have been developed that vary in taste and color, although all are an acquired taste. In China it has traditionally been used in medicine, and both the seeds and oil are used for a wide variety of health-promoting purposes.

In Japan, perilla is a commonplace ingredient in restaurants, where it is known as *shiso*, and is usually served fresh with sashimi (sliced raw fish), while in the United States and Europe perilla is becoming increasingly more available in restaurants, such is the popularity of sushi bars all over the world. It is still, however, only available to buy in specialist Asian stores.

HEALTH BENEFITS: Perilla is rich in dietary fiber and minerals such as calcium, iron, potassium and vitamins A, C and riboflavin. Perilla leaves have anti-inflammatory properties, and the herb is a well-known anti-oxidant. It is also know to help lower (bad) cholesterol. Shiso tea, made from the leaves, is thought to improve skin conditions.

Decorative and edible, purple perilla has spicy cinnamon-scented leaves that are used in Japanese cuisine.

SASHIMI OF YELLOWTAIL WITH PERILLA LEAVES

8 oz sashimi-grade yellowtail,
 sliced
1 tsp wasabi paste
¾ cup soy sauce
Perilla leaves

Arrange the sliced yellowtail on a platter lined with the perilla leaves. Serve with a dipping sauce made from the wasabi paste and soy sauce mixed together.

In Japan, perilla leaves are used as a base from which to serve sashimi.

or Hamburg parsley is popular in Central and Eastern European cuisines, where it is treated as a vegetable.

Today, parsley is widely used in kitchens throughout the world and no cook worth his salt would be without a good supply. Parsley is used in salads, stews, soups and casseroles and goes particularly well with fish; it is the herb most often used to garnish other foods. It grows best in moist, well-drained soils and thrives on plenty of sunshine.

The use of parsley dates back to ancient Greece, the name deriving from the Greek word for 'rock celery' (parsley is related to celery).

Parsley is highly nutritious and is available all-year-round; it should be washed carefully before use to dislodge dust and dirt, but must be handled carefully to avoid damaging it.

Parsley is a natural breath-freshener, reducing mouth odor, when freshly chewed, due to its high chlorophyll content.

HEALTH BENEFITS:
Good for urinary tract infections, kidney stones, gastrointestinal disorders, constipation, jaundice, flatulence, indigestion, colic, diabetes, coughs, asthma, fluid retention, anemia, high blood pressure. Said to be an aphrodisiac, it has good amounts of vitamin C.

PARSLEY

BOTANICAL NAME: *Petroselinum crispum* and *P. c. neapolitanum*
FAMILY: Apiaceae

Curly-leafed parsley (*petroselinum crispum*) and flat-leafed parsley (*P. c. neapolitanum*) are biennials native to the central Mediterranean region but which have become widely naturalized in other parts of the world. Root

COD IN PARSLEY SAUCE

½ cup skimmed milk

2 cod fillets

2 tsp butter

1½ tbsp all-purpose flour

2 tbsp vegetable or fish stock

4 tbsp finely-chopped parsley

Lemon wedges

Salt and pepper

Serves 2

1 Heat the milk in a skillet, then add the cod fillets, cover, and poach gently for about 5 minutes.

2 Transfer the cod fillets to a plate and keep warm. Reserve the poaching milk.

3 In a saucepan, melt the butter. Add the flour and cook over a low heat for 2 minutes. Remove from the heat, then whisk in the hot milk, stock, chopped parsley, salt and pepper. Return to a low heat and cook, stirring constantly, for about 3 minutes, until the sauce thickens.

4 Plate up the fish with the parsley sauce poured over. Serve with a green vegetable and lemon wedges to garnish.

PEA SHOOTS

Botanical name: *Pisum sativum*
Family: *Fabaceae*

The pea is a commonly eaten vegetable, being the small, spherical seed or seed pod of *Pisum sativum*. Peas are a cool-season crop, generally grown in temperate climates; in early times, in the Mediterranean region, they would have been gathered from the wild but, as with so many other wild foods, it became expedient to cultivate them.

While the humble pea is mostly popular for its seed, pea shoots are also a tasty and nutritious modern variation on a theme. Pea shoots are the young leaves and tips of the vines of the pea plant, which today can be found in most stores, farmers' markets, and specialist Asian grocery stores.

Pea shoots are mild in flavor with a mild pea taste. In Asian cooking they are commonly stir-fried combined with other vegetables, garlic and ginger.

In salads the shoots are crisp and juicy and can be combined with or replace other salad leaves.

Health benefits: Pea shoots, like many other leafy vegetables, are incredibly nutritious., being rich in vitamins C, A, E, thiamine, riboflavin and B6. They are full of phytonutrients and are important as an antioxidant.

PEA-SHOOT SALAD

3 handfuls pea shoots, thoroughly
 washed
½ cup cooked, chopped ham
¼ cup shredded beetroot
¼ cup podded and cooked broad
 beans
1 cup sugar snap peas

Vinaigrette Dressing:
3 tbsp extra virgin olive oil
2 tbsp white wine vinegar
1 tsp Dijon mustard
Salt and pepper

Serves 2

Mix the salad ingredients together
in a bowl. In a separate jug, mix
up the vinaigrette, then serve the
salad immediately with a drizzle
of the dressing poured over.

LAVER

BOTANICAL NAME: *Porphyra umbilicalis*
FAMILY: *Bangiaceae*

Laver is an edible, littoral alga (seaweed) with a high content of dietary minerals, iodine and iron in particular. It is consumed all over East Asia where it is known as *zicai* in China, *nori* in Japan and *gim* in Korea. In Wales, it is used to make a traditional Welsh dish known as laverbread, eaten with bacon and cockles (clams), while in Ireland it is known as slake.

Asian laver is usually sold in flat sheets and is often roasted or used in the preparation of sushi. The word *nori* started to be used widely in the United States, and the product (imported in dry form from Japan) became widely available in the 1960s, due to the influence of the macrobiotic movement, and in the 1970s with the growing number of sushi bars and Japanese restaurants in the USA.

HEALTH BENEFITS: Laver contains a variety of healthy nutrients. It is an excellent fiber source, thought to have anticancer and detoxifying properties. It benefits diabetes, digestive problems, the teeth, the cardiovascular system and the skin and eyes.

LEFT & ABOVE: Laver, when dried, can be used as an ingredient to add beneficial nutrients and flavor to other foods.

OPPOSITE: Laver grows on rocks along the seashore. It can be found growing in temperate zones all over the world.

SUSHI ROLLS WITH SALMON & CUCUMBER

2 sheets nori

4 oz skinless salmon fillets,
 poached and cut into small
 pieces.

¼ cucumber, deseeded and thinly
 sliced lengthways

¼ avocado, thinly sliced

Squeeze of wasabi paste

3 tbsp pickled ginger

Soy sauce

For the rice:

¾ cup sushi rice

2 tsp saké

1 tbsp superfine sugar

1 tbsp rice vinegar

Makes 12 rolls

1 Rinse the sushi rice in a colander, massaging it with your hands until the water runs clear, then leave to drain for 15 minutes.

2 Place the rice in a saucepan with 1¼ cups water and the saké. Bring to a boil, then cover with a lid. Reduce the heat to low and simmer for 20 minutes or until the liquid is absorbed. Remove from the heat and set aside for a further 20 minutes with the lid on.

3 In a large bowl, dissolve the sugar in the vinegar with a good pinch of salt. Add the rice and mix thoroughly. Cover with a damp cloth and set aside at room temperature until ready to use.

4 Place 1 nori sheet on a bamboo mat and cover the surface with half the cooled rice. Lay half the salmon, cucumber (use a vegetable peeler to slice it) and avocado slices along the length of the rice in a strip, being careful not to overfill. Run a pea-sized blob of wasabi (more if you like plenty of heat) along the edge of the filling, spreading it with your finger.

5 With the help of the mat, roll the sushi up tightly and squeeze to seal when you reach the end. Repeat with the remaining nori, salmon, cucumber and avocado and more wasabi. Slice each roll into 6 pieces and serve with extra wasabi, the pickled ginger and the soy sauce. Will keep in the fridge for a day.

RADISH GREENS

BOTANICAL NAME: *Raphanus sativus*
FAMILY: *Brassicaceae*

The radish is generally used as a root vegetable. Other names include European radish, spring radish and summer radish. It is thought to have originated in South-East Asia where wild forms were first discovered.

Its domestication dates back to ancient Greece and Rome where it was cultivated as a crop. Radishes are grown for their swollen tap-roots which can be globular to tapering in shape. The skins range in color from pink, red, purple to yellow and white. The flesh is crisp and sweet, but can become bitter if allowed to stay in the ground for too long.

Today, radishes are popular throughout the world and are available at all mainstream stores and supermarkets. The greens or tops, however, are invariably discarded when the radishes are offered for sale, or thrown onto the compost heap. This is unfortunate because they are a perfectly good food source and somewhat surprisingly contain six times more vitamin C than the root. The leaves themselves are peppery, pleasantly sharp and slightly bitter, and can be cooked like other types of greens or used in salads or sandwiches. They are also excellent in stir-fries or added to soups.

HEALTH BENFITS: Radishes are good for the metabolism and benefit blood circulation, headaches, constipation, nausea, obesity, respiratory diseases, gall stones, diabetes and dyspepsia. They are rich in vitamins C and B-complex, and contain many minerals and nutrients, including phosphorus, potassium and zinc.

212

SWISS CHARD, RADISH GREENS & POTATO SOUP

⅓ cup extra virgin olive oil

1 large onion

4 cloves garlic, crushed

1½ lbs potatoes, peeled and sliced

5 packed cups chopped Swiss chard leaves

1 packed cup chopped radish greens

Salt and freshly ground pepper

Serves 6

1 Place the oil, onion and garlic in a large stockpot and sauté the vegetables over a low heat until they are soft and translucent (do not brown). Add the potatoes and 8 cups of water and bring to a boil. Add a little salt and cook for about 15 minutes until the potatoes are nearly soft.

2 Add the chard and radish greens with 2 tbsp olive oil. Bring back to a simmer and cook for about 5 minutes until the leaves wilt. Check that the soup is salty enough and serve, sprinkled with freshly ground pepper.

SORREL

BOTANICAL NAME: *Rumex acetosa*
FAMILY: *Polygonaceae*

Sorrel is otherwise known as common sorrel, spinach dock and narrow-leaved dock, being a perennial herb in the Polygonaceae family. The leaves are the food of the larvae of several species of Lepidoptera, including the blood-vein moth.

Garden sorrel has been cultivated for hundreds of years. It is usually found in grassland habitats growing wild, but can be easily cultivated in the garden or grown in pots. The leaves are sharp in taste, reminiscent of wild strawberries and very astringent, making it something of an acquired taste.

The leaves can be cooked in soups and sauces or used raw in salads. Sorrel has a high oxalic acid content, which is a poison whose intake should be regulated. In small quantities, however, it is quite harmless.

HEALTH BENEFITS: Of benefit to the eyes, the immune system, the digestion, bones, the circulation, and skin. It boosts energy levels and is known to be beneficial to those with diabetes, heat problems and kidney disease. Contains vitamins A and C and many other valuable nutrients and minerals.

216

SORREL & THYME SOUP

2 tbsp butter

1 onion, roughly chopped

8 oz potatoes, peeled and roughly
 chopped

1 tbsp chopped thyme leaves

8 oz sorrel leaves, washed and
 shredded

3¾ cups chicken or vegetable
 stock

¾ cup heavy cream

Salt and pepper

Serves 2–3

1 Heat the butter in a large pot and sauté the onion until it is soft and translucent.

2 Add the potatoes, half the thyme, sorrel and stock. Bring to a boil and simmer gently for about 20 minutes or until the potatoes are very soft.

3 Cool slightly, then use a stick blender to process the soup. Pass the soup through a sieve for an extra smooth result and return to the pot.

4 Add the cream and the seasonings to taste and reheat without boiling. (If the soup is still too thick, add further stock or milk at this point.) Serve with a few chopped sorrrel leaves scattered on top.

SAGE

BOTANICAL NAME: *Salvia officinalis*
FAMILY: *Lamiaceae*

Sage, also called garden sage or common sage, is a perennial, evergreen subshrub with woody stems, greyish-green leaves, and blue to purplish flowers. It is a member of the mint family, Lamiaceae, and is native to the Mediterranean region, although it has become naturalized in many other parts of the world.

Sage has a long history of medicinal and culinary use and as an ornamental garden plant. The Latin name is thought to derive from *salvere*, to save, indicating the medical value of the plant, which has been variously used since ancient times to ward off evil, for snakebite, and to increase the fertility of women.

Several Central American sages have sweet, fruity flavors that are very different from those of Mediterranean sage, e.g., pineapple sage (*Salvia rutilans*), peach sage (*Salvia greggii*), fruit sage (*Salvia dorisiana*) and more. Also native to Central America is the hallucinogenic *Salvia divinorum* (sacred sage, sage of the seers), which was cultivated by native peoples and used in religious ceremonies before the arrival of the Spanish conquistadors.

Sage is used to enhance the flavor of meats, such as chicken, turkey and pork, and often appears in stuffings. It is easily available in mainstream stores and supermarkets.

HEALTH BENEFITS: Used as a stimulant, astringent, antiseptic for sore throats, mouth ulcers, gum disease, tonsillitis, muscle spasm, sedative, menopausal night sweats and hot flushes (flashes), infertility.

RAVIOLI WITH SAGE & BUTTER SAUCE

1 15-oz package fresh ravioli

2 tbsp butter

1 tbsp olive oil

10 sage leaves

Squeeze lemon juice

Salt and pepper

4 tbsp grated Parmesan cheese

Serves 4

1 Cook the ravioli according to the package instructions. Drain and keep warm.

2 Heat the butter and the oil in a skillet set over a medium heat until the butter melts. Add the sage leaves, swirling them briefly in the butter.

3 Add the ravioli and a squeeze of lemon juice, and fold into the butter and sage mixture. Heat through gently but thoroughly. Season with salt and pepper, adding a sprinkling of grated Parmesan cheese to serve.

SPINACH

BOTANICAL NAME: *Spinacia oleracea*
FAMILY: *Amaranthaceae (previously Chenopodiaceae)*

Spinach is an edible flowering plant native to Persia, or modern Iran, where its use was documented for the first time in AD 226. Arab traders were probably responsible for its spread throughout Asia and, over the centuries, it was slowly introduced to the rest of the world, with the result that it is possibly the most widely used vegetable in the world today.

Bright and vibrant in appearance, spinach is not only appealing to the eye but is also extremely healthy to eat. There are many different ways to enjoy this leafy vegetable, but one of the best is to sauté it lightly and briefly in butter, oil and garlic, seasoning it with salt and pepper. On no account must it be overcooked.

Spinach can also be eaten raw, when it is young enough to be tender. It has a bittersweet taste and its color is so strong that it can be used to dye pasta green. When used in salads, spinach is often combined with tomatoes, walnuts and cheese, particularly feta or haloumi. It is also used in Asian cooking and is delicious in omelets and frittatas.

Spinach grows best in temperate climates, with the United States and the Netherlands being its largest producers.

HEATH BENEFITS: Spinach is known to be one of the most nutritious foods available, being rich in vitamins A, C and K, manganese, folate and magnesium and other measurably important nutrients. It is high in antioxidants, possibly helping to prevent numerous cancers, and improves cardiovascular health. It is also known to aid brain function and has anti-aging properties. Spinach is also high in dietary fiber, which aids digestion, prevents constipation and helps to control blood sugar levels.

SPINACH & POTATO FRITTATA

1 lb baby spinach leaves, very
 thoroughly washed
9 large eggs
1 tbsp milk
⅓ cup grated Parmesan cheese
2 tbsp olive oil
1 medium onion, finely chopped
1 clove of garlic, finely chopped
5 large potatoes, boiled and cut
 into slices
Salt and freshly ground black
 pepper

Serves 4

1 Preheat the oven to 400F. Cook the spinach in ¼ cup of water until just wilted. Rinse with cold water to cool and drain. Wrap the spinach in paper towels and squeeze out as much moisture as possible, then chop and set aside.

2 In a mixing bowl, whisk the eggs, milk and Parmesan cheese together. Set aside.

3 Sauté the onion in the olive oil in a heavy, non-stick, ovenproof skillet until golden but not too brown. Add the garlic and potato slices and cook for a further minute or so. Mix the chopped spinach in with the onions and garlic.

4 Evenly spread the spinach and potato mixture over the bottom of the skillet, then pour over the reserved egg mixture. As it cooks, use a spatula to lift up the edges of the frittata, allowing the egg mixture that is still liquid to flow underneath. When it is still half cooked, place the frittata in the oven for about 15 minutes to complete the cooking and brown the top. Cut into four portions. Can be served hot or cold.

DANDELION GREENS

BOTANICAL NAME: *Taraxacum officinale*
FAMILY: *Asteraceae*

The English word 'dandelion' was first seen in its written form in 1363. The word, however, comes from the Old French *dent-de-lion* (which refers to the serrated, tooth-like edges of its leaves).

This is a flowering plant previously native to Europe and Asia but which is now commonly seen in many countries of the world. The dandelion has a distinctive yellow flower head, and fruits in the form of ball-shaped gossamer clusters of wind-dispersed seeds.

Dandelions are a familiar sight in grassy areas, lawns, roadsides and scrubland. Many gardeners regard them as weeds and dig them up, but they persist in making their presence felt.

While the dandelion is regarded as a weed by most gardeners, it does have several culinary uses, and the specific name *officinalis* refers to its valuable properties as a medicinal herb.

Dandelion leaves (alternatively dandelion greens), probably closest in character to mustard greens, can be eaten boiled or raw in various forms, such as in soups or salads. The raw leaves have a slightly bitter but pleasant taste, and a salad of them is often accompanied by hard-cooked eggs.

HEATH BENEFITS: Anti-cariogenic (prevents decay), diuretic, of benefit to those with anemia or diabetes, lowers (bad) cholesterol and blood pressure, good for urinary problems. An excellent supplement for pregnant and post-menopausal women. May also help acne sufferers.

DANDELION & EGG SALAD

Dandelion leaves

4 medium-sized, boiled potatoes, cut into chunks

4 hard-boiled eggs, sliced

4 rashers of bacon, fried until crisp and crumbled into small pieces

Serves 4

Nicely arrange all the ingredients on individual plates, drizzle with a light vinaigrette, and serve.

230

NETTLE

Botanical name: *Urtica dioica*
Family: *Urticaceae*

The nettle, stinging nettle or common nettle is an herbaceous perennial flowering plant, native to Europe, Asia, North Africa and North America, and is the best-known member of the family Urticaceae. The plant's leaves and stems are well-equipped with stinging hairs, called trichomes, which act like hypodermic needles, injecting histamines and other chemicals that produce a stinging sensation in the skin when touched by human beings and other animals.

The plant has a long history of use as a medicine and as a food source. Nettles are usually found in the countryside, but the plant is restricted by its need for moist soil. As well as the potential for encouraging beneficial insects, nettles have a number of other uses in the vegetable garden. The stinging nettle has a flavor similar to that of spinach and cucumber when cooked (and rendered harmless) and it is rich in vitamins and minerals.

Nettles may be used in a variety of recipes, in polenta, pesto, teas and purées. Nettle soup is particularly delicious.

Health benefits: Useful as an astringent, expectorant, tonic, anti-inflammatory, diuretic, beneficial for kidney health, arthritic or rheumatic conditions, allergies, anemia and kidney disease. Its use as an anti-dandruff shampoo may also stimulate hair growth. Contains beta-carotene, vitamins A, C and E, iron, calcium, phosphates and minerals.

Caution: Always use gloves when picking stinging nettles. Once cooked or dried, however, and they are rendered harmless.

NETTLE SOUP

4 tbsp lard or bacon fat

⅓ cup rolled oats

2 leeks, washed and sliced

8 oz young nettle tops, thoroughly
 washed

12 oz potatoes, peeled and
roughly diced

1½ pints vegetable or chicken
 stock

½ pint milk

Salt and freshly ground black
 pepper

Serves 6–8

1 Heat the fat in a large pot and sauté the oats until they begin to turn golden at the edges.

2 Add the leeks, nettles and potatoes and sauté for a few minutes more until the nettles wilt. Then add the stock, milk and seasonings and bring to a boil.

3 Simmer for 30 minutes, stirring occasionally, until all the vegetables are tender. Check the seasonings and process the soup in a blender, if you wish. Drizzle with olive and serve the soup with warm soda bread or potato cakes.

LAMB'S LETTUCE

Botanical name: *Valerianella locusta*

Family: *Caprifoliaceae*

Lamb's lettuce, also known as mâche, feldsalat, corn salad or fetticus, is a commonly used salad ingredient which is dark green in color and soft in texture with a characteristic nutty flavor. In parts of Europe, Africa and Asia it grows wild and is regarded as a weed, while in North America it escaped while being cultivated and has now become naturalized. In France it is cultivated on a large scale where it is then sold to many other European countries.

Lamb's lettuce must be harvested with care due its fragile nature and it is consequently an expensive salad to buy. It is always served fresh due to its tender nature, never cooked. It is at its best in spring and early summer and goes well with other salad ingredients, eggs and various cheeses.

Lamb's lettuce grows in a low rosette with spatulate leaves. It gets its name from the fact that its leaves bear a resemblance to a lamb's tongue.

There are two main varieties; curly lamb's lettuce, which has round leaves, and blond lamb's lettuce which has longer, spoon-shaped leaves.

Health benefits: The leaves are very nutritious in that they contain large amounts of vitamins B1 and C, and are also rich in calcium, magnesium, potassium, iron, zinc and dietary fiber. Historically, lamb's lettuce has been used to treat anxiety, depression and lack of energy.

LAMB'S LETTUCE, EGG, RADISH, CUCUMBER & SOFT CHEESE ON TOAST

2 slices of toast
1 hard-cooked egg, peeled and sliced
4 slices cucumber
4 sprigs lamb's lettuce
2 tbsp cream cheese
2 radishes, sliced

Serves 2

Spread the cheese evenly over the toast and cover layers of lamb's lettuce. Then add layers of cucumber, then radish, then the egg and finally with a garnish of the lamb's lettuce. Serve immediately.

SMOOTHIES

Smoothies are often recommended to health-conscious people with such additions as soy milk, whey powder, green tea, herbal or nutritional supplement mixes. It follows, therefore, that smoothies made from leafy greens, which are nutritional powerhouses in themselves, are a cheap and effective way of transferring their many benefits to your body, and can be mixed with other fruits and vegetables to make them more palatable and interesting.

Other health-boosting ingredients, such as nuts, seeds or avocado may also be added to give a healthy protein and fat injection to your smoothie, turning it into a complete, well-balanced meal.

Smoothie machines/blenders all operate differently, so follow the manufacturers' instructions to get the best results.

GREEN TEA & MINT SMOOTHIE

1 cup strong green tea, left to cool

2 cups milk (dairy-free soy or
 coconut milk may be substituted)

½ cup mint leaves

¼ cup maple syrup

1 tsp vanilla extract

¼ tsp mint extract

Serves 2

1 Put all the ingredients into a blender, cover, and process until smooth.

2 Place in the freezer and leave until partially frozen.

3 Return to the blender and remix until smooth. Serve over ice.

KALE, LETTUCE, APPLE & LIME SMOOTHIE

3 cups pure apple juice

¾ cup chopped kale leaves (ribs and stems removed)

¾ cup chopped romaine lettuce

Juice of 1 lime

¾ cup ice cubes

Serves 2

Place everything in the blender, cover, and process until smooth and frothy.

SPINACH, BANANA & KIWI SMOOTHIE

1 large banana

1 cup spinach

2 kiwi fruit, peeled

2 cups milk

3 tsp honey

¾ cup ice cubes

Serves 2

Put all the ingredients into a blender and process until smooth.

CELERY & AVOCADO SMOOTHIE

1 avocado (peeled and with pit removed)

½ small lemon, peeled and deseeded

2 medium stalks celery (washed and sliced)

1 apple (peeled and chopped)

3-4 ice cubes

1 cup coconut milk

A little honey or sugar to taste (optional)

Serves 2

Put everything into a blender, cover, and process until smooth.

MINT, COCONUT & APPLE SMOOTHIE

A handful of mint leaves

1 cup coconut milk

1½ cups apple juice

½ cup ice cubes

Serves 2–3

Put everything into a blender, cover, and process until smooth and creamy.

LAMB'S LETTUCE, CUCUMBER & PEAR SMOOTHIE

1 cucumber, peeled and chopped
2 pears, peeled, cored and
  chopped
2 cups finely chopped lamb's
  lettuce
½ cup water

½ cup plain yogurt

Serves 2

Put the cucumber, pears, water and yogurt into the blender and process until smooth. Add the chopped lamb's lettuce and mix well. Chill and serve.

BROCCOLI & ORANGE SMOOTHIE

4 broccoli florets

2 oranges (peeled and quartered)

1 carrot (chopped)

½ cucumber, peeled and chopped

1–2 cups water

Serves 2

Put everything into the blender, cover, and process until smooth. Serve chilled.

BASIL & STRAWBERRY SMOOTHIE

2 cups frozen strawberries

2 tbsp freshly squeezed lime juice

1 tbsp finely chopped basil
 leaves

2 cups coconut milk

½ cup ice cubes

Sugar or honey to taste

Serves 2

Blend all the ingredients and partially freeze them. Blend again before drinking.

CELERY, APPLE & LIME SMOOTHIE

2 medium stalks celery (washed
 and sliced)
2 apples (peeled and chopped)
Juice of 1 lime
3-4 ice cubes
2 cups coconut milk
Honey or sugar to taste, optional

Serves 2

Put everything into the blender,
cover, and process until smooth

SPINACH, APPLE & LIME SMOOTHIE

1 heaped cup spinach leaves

1 cup milk

2 drops vanilla extract

1 frozen banana

½ apple, peeled and chopped

Juice of 1 lime

1 tsp of honey

Serves 2

1 Blend together the spinach, milk and vanilla.

2 Add the frozen banana, apple, lime juice and honey and blend until smooth.

ACKNOWLEDGEMENTS

All images supplied by © Shutterstock.com other than the
following: © istockphoto.com and the following photographers.
Page 175 ajafoto, page 137 A_Lein, page 202 left alexfiodrorov, page
166 AmandaLiza, page AnjelaGr page 99 audaxl audaxl, pages 229
Basmeelker, pages 83, 224 bedo, page 81 bhofack2, page 145 CaronB,
page 181 cerealphotos, page 169 chiuinhaolo, page 178 Christian-
Fischer, page 173 coramueller, page 58 dsblock, page 228 egal, page
108 Elenathewise, page 170 ffolas, page 187 GrishaL, page 189
hawk111, page 111 hhiropi, page 113 ivandzyuba, page 61 Jess311,
page 188 Liewy, page 232 Lenushka2012, page 60 Lupidloop, page 9
michaelschott, page 172 Oliver Hoffmann, page 180 marilyna, page
182 melpomeneum, pages 184, 186 natashamum, page 136 onairda,
page pabkov, page 112 papkin, Page 140 PhilippeDesoche, page 147
Pico, page 82 pkdirector, pages 110, 118 PicturePartners, page 233
Salahudin, page 144 Scisettalfio, page 5 Seandnad, page 177
Sebastian Sinemus, page 168 Skystorm, page 225 SylvieBouchard,
page 106 Tomboy2290, page 234 Vaivirga, page 5 Violletta, page 187
right Zia-shusha.